LAWS AND LEGISLATION

THE FOURTH AMENDMENT: SELECT ISSUES AND CASES

Laws and Legislation

Additional books in this series can be found on Nova's website under the Series tab.

Additional E-books in this series can be found on Nova's website under the E-book tab.

LAWS AND LEGISLATION

THE FOURTH AMENDMENT: SELECT ISSUES AND CASES

JESSE V. KESSLER
EDITOR

Nova Science Publishers, Inc.
New York

For permission to use material from this book please contact us:
Telephone 631-231-7269; Fax 631-231-8175
Web Site: http://www.novapublishers.com

Additional color graphics may be available in the e-book version of this book.

LIBRARY OF CONGRESS CATALOGING-IN-PUBLICATION DATA

The Fourth Amendment : select issues and cases / editors, Jesse V. Kessler.
p. cm.
Includes index.
ISBN 978-1-61728-885-2 (hardcover)
1. Searches and seizures--United States. 2. United States. Constitution.
4th Amendment. I. Kessler, Jesse V.
KF9630.A25 2010
345.73'0522--dc22

2010026979

Published by Nova Science Publishers, Inc. † New York

CONTENTS

PREFACE

The Fourth Amendment of the U.S. Constitution requires government-conducted searches and seizures to be supported by probable cause and a warrant. Federal courts have long recognized that there are many exceptions to these requirements, one of which is the border search exception. The border search exception permits government officials to conduct "routine" searches based on no suspicion of wrongdoing whatsoever. On the other hand, when warrantless border searches are particularly invasive, and thus "non-routine", they are permissible only when customs officials have, at a minimum, a "reasonable suspicion" of wrongdoing. This book examines the Fourth Amendment of the U.S. Constitution as it relates today to border security, government access to phone calling activity and related records, student strip searches, and governmental drug testing and compulsory DNA collection from people who have been convicted on criminal charges.

Chapter 1 - The Fourth Amendment requires that a search or seizure conducted by a governmental agent be reasonable and supported by probable cause. The Supreme Court has interpreted the Fourth Amendment to include a presumptive warrant requirement on all searches and seizures conducted by the government. Any violation of these requirements could result in the suppression of any information derived therefrom. The Supreme Court, however, has also recognized situations that render obtaining a warrant impractical or against the public's interest and has accordingly crafted various exceptions to the warrant and probable cause requirements of the Fourth Amendment.

Few exceptions to the presumptive warrant and probable cause requirements are more firmly rooted than the "border search" exception. Derived from the sovereign right to stop and examine persons and property crossing into the country, border searches allow customs officials the flexibility to inspect incoming individuals and their belongings and to interdict incoming contraband without having to inform a magistrate before the search.

Border searches can also occur in places other than the actual physical border. Two different legal concepts authorize such searches: (1) searches at the functional equivalent of the border; and (2) extended border searches. These concepts allow federal officers to conduct border searches even in situations when it is not feasible to conduct the search at the actual point of entry (e.g., examining a person upon arrival at a U.S. airport rather than during a mid-flight crossing into the country).

Courts have determined that border searches usually fall into two categories—routine and nonroutine—though this analysis may no longer apply to searches of vehicles or personal property. Generally, the distinction between "routine" and "non-routine" turns on the level of intrusiveness. Routine border searches are reasonable simply by virtue of the fact that they occur at the border and consist of only a limited intrusion, while non-routine searches generally require "reasonable suspicion" and vary in technique and intrusiveness.

This report first outlines the statutes authorizing certain federal officers to conduct warrantless searches: 19 U.S.C. § 482 for customs officials and Immigration and Nationality Act (INA) § 287 (codified in 8 U.S.C. § 1357) for immigration officers. It then addresses the scope of the government's constitutional authority to search and seize persons and property at the border. It also describes the varying levels of suspicion generally required for each type of border search as interpreted by the courts. Finally, this report lists several bills before the 111th Congress that address border searches: two of which, H.R. 239 (the Securing our Borders and our Data Act of 2009) and H.R. 1726 (the Border Security Search Accountability Act of 2009), address border searches of laptops and other electronic storage devices. H.R. 1900 would provide emergency deployments of federal officers to the border and would authorize funds to local law enforcement to stem the illegal trafficking of firearms into Mexico. S. 205, H.R. 495, and H.R. 1448 would also authorize funds for Bureau of Alcohol, Tobacco, Firearms, and Explosives agents to interdict the illegal trafficking of firearms to Mexico.

This report does not address interior searches and seizures performed by immigration personnel since they are not traditional "border searches."

Chapter 2 - As a general rule, the Fourth Amendment of the U.S. Constitution requires government-conducted searches and seizures to be supported by probable cause and a warrant. Federal courts have long recognized that there are many exceptions to these requirements, one of which is the border search exception. The border search exception permits government officials to conduct "routine" searches based on no suspicion of wrongdoing whatsoever. On the other hand, when warrantless border searches are particularly invasive, and thus "non-routine," they are permissible only when customs officials have, at a minimum, a "reasonable suspicion" of wrongdoing.

The federal courts that have addressed this issue have held that the border search exception applies to searches of laptops at the border. Although the Supreme Court has not directly addressed the degree of suspicion needed to search laptops at the border without a warrant, the federal appellate courts that have addressed the issue appear to have concluded that reasonable suspicion is not needed to justify such a search. The Ninth Circuit, in *United States v. Arnold*, explicitly held that reasonable suspicion is not required to conduct a warrantless search of a laptop at the border.

Customs and Border Protection (CBP) and Immigration and Customs Enforcement (ICE), two agencies within the Department of Homeland Security (DHS) that have roles in border security, have published directives outlining their policies and procedures regarding laptop border searches. Both policies assert that, as a general matter, laptop border searches may be conducted without any individualized suspicion and require reasonable suspicion only in certain circumstances.

A bill introduced in the 111th Congress, the Securing our Borders and our Data Act of 2009 (H.R. 239), would impose more rigorous standards for laptop searches than those the federal courts have determined are constitutionally required. Another bill introduced in the 111th Congress, the Border Security Search Accountability Act of 2009 (H.R. 1726), would mandate that the Commissioner of Customs and Border Protection promulgate a rule with respect to the scope of and procedural and record keeping requirements associated with border security searches of electronic devices.

Chapter 3 - Public interest in the means by which the government may collect telephone call records has been raised by ongoing revelations regarding alleged intelligence activity by the National Security Agency (NSA) and the Federal Bureau of Investigation (FBI). According to a *USA Today* article from May 11, 2006, the NSA allegedly sought and obtained records of telephone numbers called and received from millions of telephones within the United States from three telephone service providers; a fourth reportedly refused to provide such records. Additionally, a series of reports issued by the Department of Justice's Office of the Inspector General (DOJ OIG), most recently in January of 2010, indicate that, between 2002 and 2006, consumer records held by telephone companies had been provided to the FBI through the use of "exigent letters" and other informal methods that fell outside of the national security letter (NSL) process embodied in statute and internal FBI policies.

The Supreme Court has held that there is no Fourth Amendment protection of telephone calling records held in the hands of third party providers, where the content of any call is not intercepted. However, this report summarizes existing *statutory* authorities regarding access by the government, for either foreign intelligence or law enforcement purposes, to information related to telephone calling patterns or practices. Where pertinent, it also discusses statutory prohibitions against accessing or disclosing such information, along with relevant exceptions to those prohibitions.

Statutory provisions authorizing, pursuant to court order, the use of pen registers and trap and trace devices exist in both the Foreign Intelligence Surveillance Act (FISA), 50 U.S.C. § 1841 *et seq.*, and, for law enforcement purposes, in 18 U.S.C. § 3121 *et seq.*

FISA's "business records" provision, 50 U.S.C. § 1861, provides authority, pursuant to court order, for requests for production of "any tangible thing" relevant to collection of foreign intelligence information not concerning a
U.S. person, or relevant to an investigation into international terrorism or clandestine intelligence activities. Under 50 U.S.C. § 1861, an investigation concerning a U.S. person may not be based solely on activities protected by the First Amendment.

Access to stored electronic communications is addressed in 18 U.S.C. § 2701 *et seq.* 18 U.S.C. § 2702 prohibits voluntary disclosure of customer communications records by a service provider unless it falls within one of several exceptions. Required disclosure of customer records to the government under certain circumstances is addressed under 18 U.S.C. § 2703, including, among others, disclosure pursuant to a warrant or grand jury or trial subpoena. 18 U.S.C. § 2709 is a national security letter provision, under which a wire or electronic service provider may be compelled to provide subscriber information and toll billing records information, or electronic communication transactional records in its custody or possession.

Finally, § 222 of the Communications Act of 1934, as amended, protects customer proprietary network information, and violations of pertinent provisions of law or regulation may expose service providers to criminal sanctions, civil penalties, and forfeiture provisions.

Public interest in the means by which the government may collect telephone call records has been raised by ongoing revelations regarding alleged intelligence activity by the National Security Agency (NSA) and the Federal Bureau of Investigation (FBI). According to a *USA Today* article from May 11, 2006, the NSA allegedly sought and obtained records of telephone numbers called and received from millions of telephones within the United States from three telephone service providers; a fourth reportedly refused to provide such records.[1] Additionally, a series of reports issued by the Department of Justice's Office of the Inspector General (DOJ OIG), most recently in January of 2010, indicate that, between 2002 and 2006, consumer records held by telephone companies had been provided to the FBI through the use of "exigent letters" and other informal methods that fell outside of the national security letter (NSL) process embodied in statute and internal FBI policies.[2] These reports also indicate that records may have been sought without demonstrating a relationship to an active investigation.[3]

This report summarizes legal authorities regarding access by the government, for either foreign intelligence or law enforcement purposes, to information related to telephone calling patterns or practices. Where pertinent, it also discusses statutory prohibitions against accessing or disclosing such information, along with relevant exceptions to those prohibitions.

Chapter 4 - The Fourth Amendment to the U.S. Constitution provides a right against "unreasonable searches and seizures." To deter the federal and state governments from violating this right, courts have developed an "exclusionary rule," which requires that evidence obtained as a result of an invalid search or seizure be excluded from use at trial.

The Supreme Court has narrowed the scope of the exclusionary rule in several cases since the late 1970s. In *United States v. Leon*, the Court created the "good-faith" exception to the exclusionary rule. The good-faith exception applies when officers conduct a search or seizure with "objectively reasonable reliance" on, for example, a warrant that is not obviously invalid but that a judicial magistrate should not have signed.

Until a 2006 case, *Hudson v. Michigan*, the Supreme Court had applied the good-faith exception only in cases in which the error creating the constitutional violation was caused by judicial or legislative actors, rather than by the police themselves. In *Hudson*, the Court applied the exception to a case in which police officers had violated the "knock and announce" rule by entering a home without waiting a sufficient period of time.

In *Herring v. United States*, a 2009 decision, the Supreme Court for the first time applied the good-faith exception to bar application of the exclusionary rule in a case involving police error regarding a warrant. A police officer in the case mistakenly identified an arrest warrant for the defendant. The Court held that evidence discovered after the subsequent arrest was admissible at trial because the officer's error was not "deliberate" and the officers involved were not "culpable."

In future cases, courts will apply the *Herring* "deliberate and culpable" test to determine whether to admit evidence obtained as a result of a search or seizure which is unconstitutional as a consequence of police error. A second impact of the *Herring* decision is a weaker constitutional footing for the exclusionary rule. Whereas judicially-created remedies have gained "constitutional status" in the context of some other constitutional rights, it appears that the exclusionary rule lacks such a grounding under the Court's current Fourth Amendment jurisprudence.

Chapter 5 - The Fourth Amendment protects individuals from unreasonable searches and seizures. What a court determines to be "reasonable" depends on the nature of the search and its underlying governmental purpose.

This report provides an analysis of the U.S. Supreme Court's 2009 decision, *Safford Unified School District #1 v. Redding*, which addressed the constitutionality of a strip search of a 13-yearold middle school student. Based on the facts of the case, the Court held that the school's search of a student's book bag and outer clothing was in accordance with the Fourth Amendment. However, as a result of a number of factual deficiencies, the search became constitutionally unreasonable when it went beyond the student's outerwear and ultimately led to the student being required to shake and pull out her bra and underwear.

For a discussion of drug testing in public schools, see CRS Report RL34624, *Governmental Drug Testing Programs: Legal and Constitutional Developments*, by David H. Carpenter.

Chapter 6 - Constitutional law on the subject of governmentally mandated drug testing is primarily an outgrowth of the Fourth Amendment prohibition on unreasonable searches and seizures. Judicial exceptions to traditional requirements of a warrant and individualized suspicion for "administrative" searches have been extended to random drug testing of public employees and school students where the government is able to demonstrate a "special need" beyond the demands of ordinary law enforcement. In the public employment setting, however, special needs analysis has largely been confined to relatively narrow circumstances directly implicating "compelling" public safety, law enforcement, or national security interests of the government. More generalized governmental concerns for the "integrity" or efficient operation of the public workplace have usually not been deemed sufficient to justify interference with the "reasonable expectation of privacy" of workers or other individuals to be tested. Additionally, warrantless, suspicionless drug testing programs that serve primarily a criminal law enforcement purpose are likely to be unconstitutional.

The constitutional parameters of "special needs" analysis is outlined in a series of Supreme Court rulings. In *Skinner v. Railway Labor Executives Association*, the U.S. Supreme Court upheld post-accident drug and alcohol testing of railway employees after major train accidents or incidents, and it approved the testing of U.S. Customs employees seeking promotion to certain "sensitive" jobs involving firearms use, drug interdiction duties, or access to classified information in *National Treasury Employees Union v. Von Raab*. These decisions established that "compelling" governmental interests in public safety or national security may, in appropriate circumstances, override constitutional objections to testing procedures by employees whose privacy expectations are diminished by the nature of their duties or workplace scrutiny to which they are otherwise subject. In *Veronia School District v. Acton*, the Supreme Court first approved of random drug testing procedures for high school student athletes, a holding that was subsequently extended, in *Board of Education of Independent School District No. 92 of Pottawatomie County v. Earls*, to permit random drug testing of students participating in non-athletic extracurricular activities. However, the Court placed limitations on the "special needs" doctrine when, in *Chandler v. Miller*, it voided a Georgia law requiring drug testing of candidates for state office for lack of a governmental need substantial enough to warrant suspicionless searches. Additionally, the Court generally has struck down drug testing policies that primarily serve criminal law enforcement purposes, such as in *Ferguson v. City of Charleston*.

Chapter 7 - Relying on different legal standards, courts have historically upheld laws authorizing law enforcement's compulsory collection of deoxyribonucleic acid (DNA) as reasonable under the Fourth Amendment to the U.S. Constitution. However, prior cases reviewed the extraction of DNA samples from people who had been convicted on criminal charges. New state and federal laws authorize the collection of such samples from people who have been arrested or detained but not convicted. On the federal level, the U.S. Department of Justice implemented this expanded authority with a final rule that took effect January 9, 2009.

Only a few courts have reviewed the constitutionality of pre-conviction DNA collection. The two federal district courts to have considered the issue applied the same Fourth Amendment test – the "general balancing" or "general reasonableness" test – but reached opposite conclusions. In *United States v. Pool*, the U.S. District Court for the Eastern District of California held that the government's interest in collecting a DNA sample from a person facing charges outweighed any intrusion of privacy. In *United States v. Mitchell*, the U.S. District Court for the Western District of Pennsylvania reached the opposite conclusion.

Points of disagreement between the two district court opinions are likely to reemerge as themes in future decisions addressing pre-conviction DNA collection. One difference is whether the defendant's status as a person facing criminal charges was viewed as impacting the scope of Fourth Amendment protection. Another is the extent to which the government was seen as having a legitimate interest in obtaining a DNA sample in particular, rather than a fingerprint or another identifier. Finally, the courts disagreed regarding the degree of the privacy intrusion caused by collecting a DNA sample. The latter questions are framed by a larger debate about the nature and role of DNA in law enforcement. For example, is a DNA sample merely a means by which to identify a person, like a fingerprint? Or does it present a greater privacy intrusion?

A few additional factors might complicate courts' analyses of DNA collection in future cases. For example, emerging scientific research suggests that the type of DNA used in forensic analysis might implicate a greater privacy intrusion than courts had previously assumed. In addition, most courts have yet to review the constitutionality of storing convicts' DNA profiles beyond the time of sentence completion.

In: The Fourth Amendment
Editors: Jesse V. Kessler
ISBN: 978-1-61728-885-2

Chapter 1

PROTECTING THE U.S. PERIMETER: BORDER SEARCHES UNDER THE FOURTH AMENDMENT

Yule Kim

SUMMARY

The Fourth Amendment requires that a search or seizure conducted by a governmental agent be reasonable and supported by probable cause. The Supreme Court has interpreted the Fourth Amendment to include a presumptive warrant requirement on all searches and seizures conducted by the government. Any violation of these requirements could result in the suppression of any information derived therefrom. The Supreme Court, however, has also recognized situations that render obtaining a warrant impractical or against the public's interest and has accordingly crafted various exceptions to the warrant and probable cause requirements of the Fourth Amendment.

Few exceptions to the presumptive warrant and probable cause requirements are more firmly rooted than the "border search" exception. Derived from the sovereign right to stop and examine persons and property crossing into the country, border searches allow customs officials the flexibility to inspect incoming individuals and their belongings and to interdict incoming contraband without having to inform a magistrate before the search.

Border searches can also occur in places other than the actual physical border. Two different legal concepts authorize such searches: (1) searches at the functional equivalent of the border; and (2) extended border searches. These concepts allow federal officers to conduct border searches even in situations when it is not feasible to conduct the search at the actual point of entry (e.g., examining a person upon arrival at a U.S. airport rather than during a mid-flight crossing into the country).

Courts have determined that border searches usually fall into two categories—routine and nonroutine—though this analysis may no longer apply to searches of vehicles or personal property. Generally, the distinction between "routine" and "non-routine" turns on the level of intrusiveness. Routine border searches are reasonable simply by virtue of the fact that they occur at the border and consist of only a limited intrusion, while non-routine searches generally require "reasonable suspicion" and vary in technique and intrusiveness.

This report first outlines the statutes authorizing certain federal officers to conduct warrantless searches: 19 U.S.C. § 482 for customs officials and Immigration and Nationality Act (INA) § 287 (codified in 8 U.S.C. § 1357) for immigration officers. It then addresses the scope of the government's constitutional authority to search and seize persons and property at the border. It also describes the varying levels of suspicion generally required for each type of border search as interpreted by the courts. Finally, this report lists several bills before the 111th Congress that address border searches: two of which, H.R. 239 (the Securing our Borders and our Data Act of 2009) and H.R. 1726 (the Border Security Search Accountability Act of 2009), address border searches of laptops and other electronic storage devices. H.R. 1900 would provide emergency deployments of federal officers to the border and would authorize funds to local law enforcement to stem the illegal trafficking of firearms into Mexico. S. 205, H.R. 495, and H.R. 1448 would also authorize funds for Bureau of Alcohol, Tobacco, Firearms, and Explosives agents to interdict the illegal trafficking of firearms to Mexico.

This report does not address interior searches and seizures performed by immigration personnel since they are not traditional "border searches."

INTRODUCTION

The United States' border policy seeks to balance the promotion of legitimate cross-border commerce and travel with its sovereign right to protect itself from terrorist activities, unlawful migration, and contraband. When formulating security initiatives regarding the border, officials must ensure that their search and seizure policies comply with the Fourth Amendment, which states: "The right of the people to be secure in their persons, houses, papers, and effects, against unreasonable searches and seizures, shall not be violated, and no Warrants shall issue but upon probable cause...." The Supreme Court has construed this language to impose a presumptive warrant requirement on all searches and seizures conducted by governmental authority. However, the Court has also recognized exceptions to the Fourth Amendment's warrant and probable cause requirements. One such exception is the "border search" exception. Based on the inherent authority of a sovereign nation to regulate who and what comes within it borders, this exception renders border searches *per se* reasonable under the Fourth Amendment simply because they occur at the border. Because they are considered *per se* reasonable, border searches can usually be conducted without a warrant or probable cause.

Federal courts have grouped border searches into two categories: routine and non-routine. Routine searches usually intrude into an individual's privacy in very limited ways. They generally consist of document checks, patdowns, or the emptying of pockets, and do not need to be justified by any suspicion of wrongdoing. Similarly, a government agent generally does not need suspicion of criminal activity before he may conduct limited inspections of cars and personal property at the border.

On the other hand, government officials may conduct certain "non-routine" searches at the border only if they have at least a "reasonable suspicion" that the searched individual is smuggling contraband or conducting other illegal activities. "Reasonable suspicion" means an officer has a particularized and objective basis for suspecting the searched individual of wrongdoing.[1] Certain non-routine search procedures are perceived to intrude and have the potential to be embarrassing or destructive. In order to prevent their excessive use, courts have held that border agents must have at least a "reasonable suspicion" of wrongdoing before they may conduct destructive searches of inanimate objects, prolonged detentions, strip searches, body cavity searches, X-ray searches, and the like. Whether reasonable suspicion is required is a fact-intensive totality of the circumstances test determined on a case-by-case basis.

Although there was some federal circuit precedent to require more than reasonable suspicion to justify some acutely intrusive forms of non-routine border searches, the Supreme Court has since warned against developing further gradations of suspicion beyond reasonable suspicion.[2] Thus, federal courts generally appear to apply only the reasonable suspicion standard when reviewing a non-routine border search.

The Ninth Circuit appears to have refocused the border search analysis to presume that searches at the border do not require reasonable suspicion. Thus, the fact-intensive analysis used to determine whether reasonable suspicion is required may no longer be a central consideration in analyzing border searches. Rather, the Ninth Circuit, at least, begins with the presumption that most border searches do not require any suspicion of wrongdoing to be justified. If, however, the case at issue involves (1) an intrusive search of the body, (2) a particularly destructive search of property, or (3) a search conducted in a particularly offensive manner, the presumption would be rebutted and "reasonable suspicion" would be required.

Statutory Authorization to Conduct Border Searches

Two statutory provisions confer border search powers on agents of the United States: 19 U.S.C. § 482, which allows customs officials to conduct searches of persons, vehicles, and mail at the border; and Immigration and Nationality Act (INA) § 287, which gives immigration officers broad powers to interrogate, detain, and search individuals and vehicles. Both statutes have been interpreted such that these agents may conduct searches and arrests at the border without warrant or probable cause. However, the exercise of these powers still must comport with the requirements of the Fourth Amendment.[3]

Customs Officials

Section 482 of Title 19 of the U.S. Code authorizes customs officials to conduct searches for unlawfully imported materials.[4] This provision specifically confers upon those customs officials who are authorized to board and search sea vessels the additional power to search "any vehicle, beast, or person" where they suspect they will discover goods subject to U.S. duties or goods whose importation is outlawed by the United States.[5] Federal courts have interpreted this to mean that customs officials are empowered to search vehicles for aliens, as well as contraband.[6] A customs official who exercises this authority to conduct a border search need not have a warrant or probable cause.[7] However, border searches must still be "reasonable" in light of the circumstances.[8]

Furthermore, customs officials may also search "any trunk or envelope, wherever found," in which they have "reasonable cause to suspect"[9] there is merchandise imported contrary to law.[10] The U.S. Supreme Court has interpreted "any trunk or envelope" to include all international mail entering the United States.[11] This means customs officials need not have probable cause, nor must they procure a warrant, to commence a search of a piece of international mail.[12] However, even though a customs official may conduct a border search of incoming international mail, the search is still "subject to the substantive limitations imposed by the Constitution," which is to say the Fourth Amendment's reasonableness requirement.[13]

Immigration Officers

Section 287 of the Immigration and Nationality Act (INA) expressly confers upon immigration officers[14] broad powers to question and detain individuals without warrant either at the border or in the interior of the United States. For example, immigration officers may, without warrant, interrogate aliens about their right to be within the United States.[15]

They may also conduct some searches without a warrant. The INA expressly authorizes immigration officers, within "a reasonable distance" from the external boundary of the United States, to search any land-based vehicle or conveyance, and any vessel within U.S. territorial waters.[16] Immigration officers can also access without warrant any private lands located within 25 miles of the U.S. border, but not dwellings, for the purpose of patrolling for aliens illegally entering the United States.[17] Moreover, the statute authorizes immigration officers to search, without warrant, a person and the personal effects in his possession, if the person seeks admission to the United States and the officer has reasonable cause to suspect that a search would disclose grounds for denying admission.[18]

Furthermore, immigration officers may arrest without warrant:

- any alien who, in the presence of the officer, is attempting to enter the United States in violation of the federal immigration laws;[19]
- any alien who the officer has a reason to believe is an alien currently within the United States in violation of the federal immigration laws;[20]
- any person for any felony regulating the admission or removal of aliens;[21]
- any person for any offense against the United States committed in the presence of the officer;[22] or
- any person for any felony if the officer has reasonable grounds to believe the person committed the felony, the arrest was made while the officer was performing duties relating to the enforcement of the federal immigration laws, there is a likelihood that the suspect would escape before a warrant can be obtained, and the officer is properly certified to make those types of arrests.[23]

Section 287 does not impose any specific limitations on any of the immigration officer's powers to search, interrogate, or arrest aliens without warrant.[24] Nonetheless, an immigration officer's powers to search, interrogate, or arrest aliens without warrant are still subject to constitutional constraints, including the Fourth Amendment requirement that all searches and seizures (i.e., interrogations and arrests) be reasonable.[25] As discussed below, the "reasonableness" of a search, interrogation, or arrest varies depending on the circumstances, which include the justifications for the search, the scope, place, and manner of the search, and whether an appropriate exception to the Fourth Amendment applies.

THE FOURTH AMENDMENT

The Fourth Amendment mandates that a search or seizure conducted by a government agent must be reasonable and that probable cause must support a warrant.[26] Although the Supreme Court has interpreted this to mean that a warrant is presumptively required along with a need for individualized suspicion of wrongdoing,[27] the Court has also recognized "specifically established exceptions" to the warrant and probable cause requirements of the Fourth Amendment.[28]

However, before taking these exceptions into consideration, a Fourth Amendment analysis begins with this inquiry: (1) whether the government action was sufficiently intrusive to constitute a "search" or "seizure" and (2) whether the intrusion was "reasonable" in light of the circumstances.[29]

Searches

A search triggers Fourth Amendment protections when (1) the individual personally held an expectation of privacy in the searched object or place and (2) society is willing to recognize that expectation as reasonable.[30] In order for the expectation of privacy to be deemed reasonable, there must be some property law or social norm that signifies that the searched object or place is closed from public intrusion.[31] For example, where the government uses a remote surveillance device not generally available for public use to explore physical activities within a "constitutionally protected area" (e.g., a home), and that area would have been otherwise undetectable without some sort of physical intrusion, the surveillance is a "search" and is presumptively unreasonable without a warrant.[32]

Seizures

Property or individuals may be seized. The Supreme Court has described a seizure of property as "some meaningful interference with an individual's possessory interests in that property."[33] An individual is "seized" when, in light of all the circumstances surrounding the incident, a government official makes a person reasonably believe that he is not at liberty to leave the official's presence.[34] A seizure of a person, therefore, can include full arrests, investigatory detentions, checkpoint stops for citizenship inquiries, and detentions of a person against his will. However, if a person consents to be interviewed by an officer, that interview is not a "seizure."[35]

Detaining a suspect after a consensual interview does not violate the Fourth Amendment if, during the course of the interview, the officer finds sufficient cause to suspect that the person committed wrongdoing. But an officer cannot construe a person's refusal to be interviewed as sufficient cause to suspect wrongdoing.[36]

An immigration officer's questioning of an individual illustrates how an encounter which may appear to be a seizure is in fact not. Merely questioning an individual about his identity, regardless of whether he is aware he can leave the officer or refuse to cooperate by not answering, is not a seizure.[37] Therefore, such questioning need not be predicated on reasonable suspicion that the individual is an alien.[38] Nonetheless, if "the circumstances are so intimidating as to demonstrate that a reasonable person would have believed he was not free to leave if he had not responded," then the encounter may be deemed a seizure.[39] When the interview becomes a seizure, either through a formal arrest or when the circumstances are such that a reasonable person would understand he could not leave, the officer must, at a minimum, have "a reasonable suspicion, based on articulable facts, that the person being questioned is, or is attempting to be, engaged in an offense against the United States or is an alien illegally in the United States."[40]

Reasonableness

Determining whether a government action is "reasonable" requires balancing the governmental interest justifying the intrusion against a person's legitimate expectation of privacy. When the government interest fails to justify its intrusion of a legitimate expectation of privacy, a violation of the Fourth Amendment occurs. This violation may result in any evidence derived from the unlawful search to be suppressed and excluded from a judicial proceeding. However, this "exclusionary rule" does not generally apply in proceedings involving the removal of aliens from the United States.[41]

THE DEFINITION OF "BORDER"

Warrantless searches are *per se* unreasonable under the Fourth Amendment, unless an established exception applies. The border search is a well-recognized and long established exception to the Fourth Amendment's probable cause and warrant requirements. In general, the border is the point where entry into the United States is first made by land from the neighboring countries of Mexico or Canada, at the place where a ship docks in the United States after having been to a foreign port, and at any airport in the country where international flights first land. Authorities at these locations may search a person entering or leaving the country, an individual's automobile, baggage, or goods, and materials imported to and exported from the country.[42] Authorized by the First Congress,[43] the border search exception has a history older than the Fourth Amendment and derives from Congress's inherent authority to regulate commerce with foreign nations and to enforce immigration laws.[44] The Fourth Amendment does not require warrants or probable cause for most stops and searches at the border because the power to control who or what comes within a nation's borders is an inherent attribute of national sovereignty.[45]

Although border searches may generally be conducted without a warrant or probable cause, they must still be reasonable.[46] Federal courts have determined that border searches usually fall into two categories—routine and non-routine, the distinction generally turning on the intrusiveness of the search. Routine border searches are reasonable simply by virtue of the fact that they occur at the border and consist of only a limited intrusion, while non-routine searches generally require reasonable suspicion and vary in technique and intrusiveness. It should be noted, however, that the Supreme Court has arguably suggested that the routine/non-routine analysis may no longer be appropriate for searches of vehicles and personal property.[47]

Functional Equivalent of the Border

The border search exception extends to those searches conducted at the "functional equivalent" of the border. The "functional equivalent" of a border is generally the first practical detention point after a border crossing or the final port-of-entry.[48] Places such as international airports within the country and ports within the country's territorial waters or stations at the intersection of two or more roads extending from the border exemplify such functional equivalents.[49]

This doctrine addresses the problem posed by the impossibility of stopping an individual for inspection who is in mid-transit when crossing the physical border. By permitting searches at the functional equivalent of the border, the doctrine permits a search to be effected at the first practicable location, namely the port-of-entry. The reasoning is that the port-of-entry is, much like a border checkpoint, the place where an individual first enters the country, and thus a search for contraband at a port-of-entry is as effective as a search at the border. [50]

A search at the border's functional equivalent is constitutionally valid when: (1) a reasonable certainty exists that the person or thing crossed the border; (2) a reasonable certainty exists that there was no change in the object of the search since it crossed the border; and (3) the search was conducted as soon as practicable after the border crossing.[51] In general, when applying this test, courts have given the "border" a geographically flexible reading because people can enter the country at points other than the actual border.[52]

Extended Border Search

The border search exception may also allow warrantless searches beyond the border or its functional equivalent. Under the "extended border search" doctrine, government officials may conduct a warrantless search beyond the border or its functional equivalent if (1) the government officials have a reasonable certainty[53] that a border was crossed or there exists a "high degree of probability" that a border was crossed; (2) they also have reasonable certainty that no change in the object of the search has occurred between the time of the border crossing and the search; and (3) they have "reasonable suspicion" that criminal activity was occurring.[54] This three-part test ensures that a significant temporal nexus still exists between the search and the suspect's border crossing.[55]

The extended border search doctrine has gained wide acceptance among the federal courts because they deem that it strikes a sensible balance between the legitimate privacy interests of the individual and the societal interests in the enforcement of border security laws.[56]

The Distinction between the Functional Equivalent of a Border and the Extended Border Search Doctrines

Although a search at the border's functional equivalent and an extended border search require similar elements, the extended border search entails a potentially greater intrusion on a legitimate expectation of privacy. Thus, an extended border search always requires a showing of "reasonable suspicion" of criminal activity, while a search at the functional equivalent of the border may not require any degree of suspicion whatsoever.

Another difference is that an extended border search takes place after the first point in time when an individual might have been stopped within the country.[57] For example, in *United States v. Teng Yang,* the Seventh Circuit upheld an extended border search that occurred at an international airport but after the defendant had already undergone an initial inspection at the designated U.S. border inspection site.[58] The court determined that "[i]t is the enforcement of the customs laws combined with the mandate of protecting the border of the United States that permits the extension of the search rights of border authorities to allow non-routine searches in areas near our nation's borders."[59]

TYPES OF SEARCHES AND SEIZURES AT THE BORDER

Courts have historically analyzed border searches based on whether they are "routine" or "non- routine." However, this type of division may no longer be appropriate for vehicular searches. And at least one court appears to have extended this analysis to searches of electronic storage devices and other containers.

The following sections examine how federal courts generally analyze border searches of persons, vehicles, and electronic storage devices.

Searches and Seizures of People

Routine Searches

In order to regulate the collection of duties and to prevent the introduction of illegal aliens and contraband into this country, Congress has granted the authority to conduct routine searches of persons and their personal belongings at the border without reasonable suspicion, probable cause, or a warrant.[60] A routine border search is a search that does not pose a serious invasion of privacy or offend the average traveler.[61] For example, a routine border search may consist of limited searches for contraband or weapons through a pat-down;[62] the removal of outer garments such as jackets, hats, or shoes, the emptying of pockets, wallets, or purses;[63] the use of a drug-sniffing dog;[64] the examination of outbound materials;[65] and the inspection of luggage.[66]

It has long been established that border crossers' reasonable expectation of privacy is lower at the border because they generally expect border guards to search persons and property for contraband. Because this is common knowledge, border crossers are put on notice when approaching a border that a search may be imminent, and thus their privacy is "less invaded by [border] searches" when they occur.[67] Thus, routine searches do not violate the Fourth Amendment simply because they occur at the border.[68] Moreover, courts consider routine border searches to be permissible because they are administered to a class of people (international travelers) and are not used to target individuals.[69]

There is no established test that determines whether a particular search procedure is routine. However, the degree of intrusiveness or invasiveness associated with the particular technique is especially indicative of whether a search is routine. The First Circuit, for example, compiled a nonexhaustive list of six factors to be considered: (1) whether the search required the suspect to disrobe or expose any intimate body parts; (2) whether physical contact was made with the suspect during the search; (3) whether force was used; (4) whether the type of search exposed the suspect to pain or danger; (5) the overall manner in which the search was conducted; and (6) whether the suspect's reasonable expectations of privacy, if any, were abrogated by the search.[70]

Non-Routine Searches

Once a search of a person's body goes beyond a limited intrusion, a court may determine that a non-routine search has occurred. Non-routine border searches may include prolonged detentions, strip searches, body cavity searches, and some X-ray examinations.[71] Destructive searches of property can also qualify as non-routine.

At the very least, it appears courts require a government official to have a "reasonable suspicion" of illegal activity to conduct a non-routine border search.[72] The reasonable suspicion standard generally requires an officer at the border to have "a particularized and objective basis for suspecting the particular person" of wrongdoing.[73] For example, in *United States v. Forbicetta*, the court found reasonable suspicion to exist where Customs officials acted on the following objective facts: the suspect (1) arrived from Bogota, Colombia, (2) was traveling alone, (3) had only one suitcase and no items requiring Customs inspection, (4) was young, clean-looking, and attractive, and (5) was wearing a loose-fitting dress.[74] These factors taken together matched the "smuggling profile" for narcotic carriers in that area, and thus, the court concluded there was a sufficient basis to conduct the search.

The Supreme Court has not enumerated the factors that should be considered when determining whether a border search is routine or non-routine.[75] This task has generally been left to lower federal courts. However, in *United States v. Montoya de Hernandez*, the Supreme Court concluded that one such standard, a "clear indication" of suspicion (i.e., a suggestion that is free from doubt), was not required by the Fourth Amendment to justify a prolonged detention in an airport.[76] The Court determined that the use of the term "clear indication" in its past jurisprudence was only meant to indicate the necessity for particularized suspicion, "rather than as enunciating a third Fourth Amendment threshold between 'reasonable suspicion' and 'probable cause.'"[77] Federal courts now view the *Montoya de Hernandez* reasoning as both a warning against using suspicion standards other than reasonable suspicion for non-routine border searches and a specific disavowal of the use of the "clear indication" standard when analyzing a border search. [78] Although some courts had previously required a "clear indication" to justify especially intrusive border searches other than prolonged detentions,[79] courts generally construe the disavowal of this standard in *Montoya de Hernandez* to apply to other invasive border searches. "Reasonable suspicion" is the standard used to justify non-routine searches.

Prolonged Detentions

Prolonged detentions may be conducted in order to verify or dispel an agent's suspicion that a traveler has committed wrongdoing. In *Montoya de Hernandez,* someone from Bogota, Columbia, suspected of smuggling drugs in her alimentary canal, refused to consent to an X-ray examination. In an attempt to verify or dispel their suspicions that she was engaged in criminal activity, Customs officers detained Ms. Montoya de Hernandez for over 16 hours and told her she could not leave until she eliminated the contents of her alimentary canal into a wastebasket.

The Court determined "that the detention of a traveler at the border, beyond the scope of a routine Customs search and inspection, is justified at its inception if Customs agents, considering all the facts surrounding the traveler and her trip, reasonably suspect that the traveler is smuggling contraband in her alimentary canal."[80] The Court concluded that it was reasonable to detain Ms. Montoya de Hernandez for the period of time necessary to verify or dispel the suspicion of the agents in these circumstances. [81] Courts have reasoned that "an otherwise permissible border detention does not run afoul of the Fourth Amendment simply because a detainee's intestinal fortitude leads to an unexpectedly long period of detention."[82] However, the Fifth Circuit in *United*

States v. Adekunle concluded that the government must, within a reasonable time (generally within 48 hours), seek a judicial determination that reasonable suspicion exists to detain a suspect for an extended period of time. [83]

There appear to be no "hard-and-fast time limits" that automatically transform what would otherwise be a routine search into a non-routine search, nor render a non-routine search conducted under the reasonable suspicion standard unconstitutional.[84] Rather, courts consider "whether the detention of [the traveler] was reasonably related in scope to the circumstances which justified it initially."[85] In order to provide perspective, the 16-hour detention in *Montoya de Hernandez* was considered a non-routine search (justifiable by reasonable suspicions),[86] while a one-hour vehicular search did not require reasonable suspicion.[87] The Second Circuit has characterized four- to six-hour-long detentions of individuals suspected of having terrorist ties as routine.[88]

Strip Searches

A strip search involves the removal of all or part of a suspect's clothing in order to effect a search. Because of the perceived offensiveness of the procedure due to the embarrassment it may inflict on the individual, reviewing courts generally require reasonable suspicion that the person is concealing contraband under his clothing before such a search is justified. [89] Often, in the course of a routine search, reasonable suspicion may arise to justify a subsequent strip search. For instance, in *United States v. Flores*, upon discovering 600 small undeclared emerald stones in the defendant's pockets during a routine search, Customs agents conducted a strip search and discovered an envelope of narcotics.[90] The court held that the prior discovery of the undeclared emeralds was sufficient to heighten suspicion to the level necessary to conduct the strip search.[91]

Body Cavity Searches

Narcotics and other contraband have often been smuggled in the body cavities of travelers, and searches into such cavities have become more commonplace. Body cavity searches may include inspections of the vagina or rectum, or the use of emetics.[92] Because of the extreme medical risks internal drug smuggling poses to the smuggler, courts have determined that body cavity searches and extraction of the drugs do not require the advance procurement of a search warrant from a magistrate.[93] Nevertheless, a border official must have reasonable suspicion that an individual is attempting to smuggle contraband inside his body for a court to uphold a warrantless body cavity search.[94]

Additionally, the manner in which the body cavity search is conducted must also be reasonable in light of the circumstances. Generally, conduct that "shocks the conscience" is inherently unreasonable.[95] Such conduct has included use of a stomach pump[96] and could potentially include medical procedures performed by nonmedical personnel.[97]

X-Ray Searches

X-ray searches of the body have also been used at the border. They raise Fourth Amendment concerns because individuals normally have a heightened expectation of privacy with respect to their person.[98] Because these searches do not constitute an actual physical invasion, however, the question becomes to what degree do X-ray searches intrude on this privacy?

The answer seems to turn, in large part, on whether an involuntary X-ray search is more akin to a strip search and thus only requires a "reasonable suspicion" for its application, or whether the intrusion is so great that it could potentially require a greater level of suspicion. In examining this issue, the Eleventh Circuit in *United States v. Vega-Barvo* determined that an X-ray search imposes only minimally on a person's dignity, less so than a strip search.[99] In reaching this conclusion, the *Vega-Barvo* court examined (1) the physical contact between the searcher and the person searched, (2) the exposure of intimate body parts, and (3) the use of force.[100] These factors helped the court examine the level of intrusiveness endured by the defendant and to conclude that the government agents, acting under a reasonable suspicion of illegal activity, properly detained and X-rayed the smuggler. The court reasoned that X-rays do not require physical contact or usually expose intimate body parts. The court also determined that "an x-ray is one of the more dignified ways of searching the intestinal cavity."[101] In general, other courts appear to agree with the Eleventh Circuit, likening X-ray searches to strip searches, and thus concluding that "reasonable suspicion" is the level of suspicion necessary to conduct an X-ray examination.[102]

Cumulative Effect of Multiple Routine Searches

Some have argued that subjecting an individual at the border to multiple routine searches during a period of detention can rise to the level of a non-routine search. This argument was raised in *Tabbaa v. Chertoff*, where the plaintiffs alleged that they were subjected to intrusive questioning, pat-down searches, the forcible spreading of their feet, and being fingerprinted and photographed, all in the course of a four- to six-hour period of detention at the border. [103] The Second Circuit first noted that, based on prior case law, "each of the individual elements of the searches was routine."[104] However, even though the court did "leave open the possibility that in some circumstances the cumulative effect of several routine search methods could render an overall search non-routine," the court did not find this particular sequence of search methods to be non- routine.[105] The decisive factor in determining whether a search is non-routine, said the court, is "the invasiveness of privacy" the search caused to the traveler, rather than the level of inconvenience. In this particular case, even taken collectively, the court found that the searches "were routine in the border context, albeit near the outer limits of what is permissible absent reasonable suspicion."[106] Thus, while in this particular circumstance, the series of searches was found to be routine, the Second Circuit left open the possibility that "the cumulative effect of several routine searches" could rise to the level of a non-routine search.[107]

Searches and Seizures of Vehicles

Although federal courts had initially analyzed vehicular border searches by evaluating whether they were routine or non-routine, a 2004 decision by the Supreme Court appears to have placed this practice into question. In *United States v. Flores-Montano*, the Supreme Court found that the dignity and privacy interests that require reasonable suspicion for highly intrusive searches of the person do not apply to vehicles being examined at the border.[108]

Prior to *Flores-Montano*, federal courts had concluded that border searches of personal property involving the use of "force" could be considered "non-routine," thus requiring reasonable suspicion in order to be justified under the Fourth Amendment.[109] In this vein, courts found that drilling a hole into personal property, such as a container or a vehicle, to explore its interior made the searches non-routine.[110]

However, the Supreme Court in *Flores-Montano* held that a border search involving the dismantling, removal, and reassembly of a vehicle's fuel tank did not require reasonable suspicion. The Court, in its reasoning, relied on what it characterized as the United States' longstanding right as a sovereign "to protect itself by stopping and examining persons and property crossing into [the] country...."[111] In light of the government's need to stem the flow of drugs smuggled across the United States' border, the Court determined that the "inherent authority to protect, and a paramount interest in protecting, its territorial integrity" amply justified the search of the vehicle.[112]

Furthermore, in upholding the suspicionless search, the Court noted that the search at issue resulted in the vehicle ultimately being reassembled, which differs significantly from a potentially destructive search that involves drilling.[113] The Court concluded that "while it may be true that some searches of property are so destructive as to require a different result, this was not one of them."[114] The Court, however, left open the question of "whether, and under what circumstances, a border search might be deemed 'unreasonable' because of the particularly offensive manner [in which] it is carried out."[115] Thus, reasonable suspicion may not be presumptively required to justify invasive vehicle searches because they do not implicate the same privacy interest as invasive searches of the human body; however, especially destructive searches of vehicles, and perhaps other forms of personal property, may require reasonable suspicion.[116]

Subsequently, federal courts have determined that the use of the routine/non-routine analysis for vehicular border searches has been "specifically refuted" by *Flores-Montano*.[117] These courts now rely on the reasoning of *Flores-Montano* to permit an array of search techniques on vehicles without requiring reasonable suspicion.[118] In *United States v. Cortez-Rocha*, for example, the Ninth Circuit held that reasonable suspicion was not required to justify the slashing of a vehicle's spare tire in order to search its interior.[119] The court examined (1) the degree of damage inflicted on the vehicle and (2) any potential effect on the safety or security of the vehicle or its passengers. It then concluded that the "disabling of a spare tire does not undermine the immediate safety of the vehicle or threaten the security of the vehicle's driver or passengers."[120] Other Ninth Circuit border search cases have upheld the drilling of a single 5/16-inch hole in the bed of a pickup truck,[121] the use of a radioactive density meter called a "Buster" to search the inside of a spare tire,[122] and the removal of an interior door panel.[123] In all of these cases, the court concluded that because safety was not compromised by the limited amount of damage inflicted on the vehicles, reasonable suspicion was not required. Concurring opinions, however, questioned whether the government needed a broad "suspicionless" search argument to prevail in these cases when the results could have been sustained on the grounds that there was reasonable suspicion to support the searches.[124]

Searches of Electronic Storage Devices

A developing issue is whether, at the border, the Fourth Amendment permits warrantless searches of the contents of laptop computers and other electronic storage devices, and if it does, whether these searches are routine or non-routine. [125] The U.S. Supreme Court has yet to address this matter. Some lower federal courts, however, have held that searches of laptops and other forms of electronic storage devices fall under the border search exception.[126] Yet, these courts have also been far more reticent in determining whether these types of searches are routine or non-routine. Instead, they have found that reasonable suspicion supported the searches, and, thus, they did not reach the question.[127] Even when a court has held that searches of electronic storage devices were routine, there has usually been an accompanying finding of reasonable suspicion to support the searches.[128] The one exception is the Ninth Circuit, which has expressly held that reasonable suspicion is not required to support a border search of an electronic storage device.[129]

In *United States v. Arnold*, the Ninth Circuit, while disregarding the traditional routine/nonroutine analysis following the Supreme Court's apparent rejection of such an analysis with respect to border searches of property, expressly held that reasonable suspicion was not required to support a border search of an electronic storage device.[130] Rather than evaluate the circumstances of the search and consider the particular characteristics of electronic storage devices, the court described the search as that of a "closed container."[131] Applying a "closed container" analysis, the court concluded that there was no material difference between a search of an electronic storage device and the search of a briefcase, purse, pocket, or pictures and film, and thus, like any border search of any "closed container," reasonable suspicion was not required.[132] According to the Ninth Circuit, the only two types of border searches of closed containers that would require reasonable suspicion are searches that involve "exceptional damage of property" or searches conducted in a "particularly offensive manner."[133] The court, in its holding, expressly concluded that nothing about an electronic storage device, such as its large storage capacity or its ability to contain personal information, renders a search of its contents inherently offensive.[134] Thus, the court held, border search at issue in *Arnold* did not require reasonable suspicion.[135]

Searches of Expressive Materials

Some have argued that border searches of letters, documents, and other forms of expressive content should require some form of individualized suspicion. This argument was raised before the Fourth Circuit in *Ickes*, where the defendant claimed that the suspicionless border search of his laptop was invalid because the First Amendment protects expressive content from at-will government perusal.[136] The Fourth Circuit rejected this argument for three reasons: (1) recognizing an expressive content exception to the border search doctrine would insulate terrorist and criminal communications from search, (2) applying such an exception in the field would be impractical for border officers who would have to determine, "on their feet," whether the expressive content they wish to search is protected by the First Amendment, and (3) a First Amendment exception for border searches would create inconsistencies with Supreme Court precedent which states that a higher standard than probable cause is not needed for ordinary searches of expressive content.[137] This reasoning was later endorsed by the Ninth Circuit in *Arnold*, which expressly adopted the Fourth Circuit reasoning.[138]

Thereafter, the Ninth Circuit, *en banc*, reaffirmed this holding in *United States v. Seljan*, which upheld the suspicionless border search of a letter which solicited sex from a child residing in the Philippines.[139] This search was found constitutionally sound even though the scope of the statute authorizing the search of the package containing the letter was limited to the interdiction of undeclared currency transported across the United States' border.[140] Indeed, the *Seljan* majority specifically cited *Ramsey*, arguably the seminal case concerning the border search doctrine, in holding that "[a]n envelope containing personal correspondence is not uniquely protected from search at the border."[141] Moreover, the court found additional justification for the search by concluding that it was not unreasonable under the circumstances because the customs official did not "read" the contents of the letter. Rather, he merely "scanned" it with his eyes, which then gave rise to the reasonable suspicion of unlawful conduct that justified a more exacting examination of the letter's contents.[142]

Although most federal circuits addressing this issue have held that expressive materials are not exempt from the border search exception, forceful countervailing arguments have been made. For example, in his dissent in *Seljan*, Judge Alex Kozinski argued that the Fourth Amendment provides heightened protections for expressive materials at the border.[143] He made two arguments to support this proposition. The first is based on the Fourth

Amendment's text, which contains a specific prohibition against the unreasonable search and seizure of "papers." Judge Kozinski argued that this specific prohibition signals the Framers' desire to insulate expressive content, and the personal thoughts contained therein, from unnecessary government search.[144] In support of this interpretation, Judge Kozinski provided an analysis where he cited *Entick v. Carrington*, an important English common law case familiar to the Framers, which rejected "the government's claim of unrestrained power to search personal papers" and held that the searches and seizures of documents violated English common law. [145] According to his analysis, the prevailing view at the time of *Entick* was that a search of private papers was every bit as intrusive as a body search, which, if accurate, would indicate that the Framers intended individualized suspicion to support a search of papers even at the border.[146] Second, Judge Kozinski also distinguished *Seljan* from past Supreme Court precedent by characterizing the border search exception as a means to facilitate the interdiction of smuggled contraband. [147] Thus, according to Judge Kozinski, the border search exception should be limited to the search of "containers," primarily for the purpose of uncovering contraband, and should not be applied to facilitate the search of expressive materials.[148]

LEGISLATIVE ACTION ON BORDER SECURITY

There are several bills before the 111th Congress that deal with border security. These bills follow several that were enacted in earlier Congresses and which significantly affected border security policy as recommended by the 9/11 Commission. The 9/11 Commission made several recommendations and observations in its Report for changes to U.S. border security operations. Most of these proposed changes involve enhancing the detection of travelers who would pose the United States harm and promoting cooperation between U.S. federal agencies and with foreign governments. The 9/11 Report emphasizes the importance of constraining and intercepting terrorist travel by using better technology and training to detect falsified documents.[149] To accomplish this end, the Commission recommended: (1) creating a strategy to combine terrorist intelligence, operations and law enforcement; (2) integrating the U.S. border security system into a larger network of screening points; (3) implementing a biometric entry-exit screening system; and (4) enhancing international cooperation, particularly with Canada and Mexico, to raise global border security standards.[150] Some of these recommendations, and others, were implemented by the 108th Congress in the 9/11 Intelligence Reform and Terrorism Prevention Act of 2004 (P.L. 108-458)—a compromise piece of legislation drawn from H.R. 10, the 9/11 Recommendations Implementation Act and S. 2845, the National Intelligence Reform Act of 2004 during conference.

Subsequently, the 109th Congress passed the 9/11 Intelligence Reform law and the FY2005 Emergency Supplemental Appropriation Act for Defense, the Global War on Terror, and Tsunami Relief (P.L. 109-13), which calls on DHS to study the technology, equipment, and personnel needed to address security vulnerabilities near the U.S. borders and to develop a pilot program to utilize or increase the use of ground surveillance technologies (e.g., video cameras, sensor technology, motion detectors) on both the northern and southern borders. The 109th Congress also passed the Secure Fence Act of 2006 (P.L. 109-367), which requires the Secretary of DHS to take all actions the Secretary determines necessary to achieve and maintain operational control over the entire international land and maritime borders of the United States. The Secretary is to use systematic surveillance and physical infrastructure enhancements, including fencing, to achieve control of the border.

The 110th Congress continued to address border security issues covered by the 9/11 Commission in the Implementing Recommendations of the 9/11 Commission Act of 2007.[151] This law attempts to modernize and strengthen the visa waiver program in INA § 217 by enhancing program security requirements through an electronic travel authorization system to collect biographical information about passengers, and extending visa-free travel privileges to nationals of countries that are cooperating with the United States in its anti-terrorism campaign. The law also authorizes: (1) a Terrorist Travel Program to monitor terrorists and prevent their entry into the United States, (2) the creation of a "model" port-of-entry program to help provide a more efficient and welcoming international arrival process at ports-of-entry, and (3) a pilot program to develop, with states, a machine-readable and tamper-proof driver's license that can be used for admission into the United States from either the Canadian or Mexican border.

In the current Congress, several additional proposals relate to border security and may have the potential to implicate Fourth Amendment concerns. These include the following:

- H.R. 1900 was introduced to provide emergency deployments of CBP, DEA, and ATF agents to the border and to authorize funds to local law enforcement to stem the illegal trafficking of firearms into Mexico. S. 205, H.R. 495, and H.R. 1448 would also authorize funds for ATF agents to interdict the illegal trafficking of firearms to Mexico.

- H.R. 239, the Securing our Borders and our Data Act of 2009, would prohibit searches of digital media devices based solely on the border search authority. Rather, border agents could only conduct searches of digital devices if they have reasonable suspicions of unlawful conduct. Border agents also would be prohibited from seizing digital devices based solely on their border search authority; some other undescribed constitutional authority would be required.
- H.R. 1726, the Border Security Search Accountability Act of 2009, would mandate that the Commissioner of Customs and Border Protection promulgate a rule with respect to the scope of and procedural and recordkeeping requirements associated with border security searches of electronic devices. The rule would require that (1) commercial information be handled in a manner consistent with all laws and regulations governing such information, (2) electronic searches be conducted in front of a supervisor, (3) the number of days commercial information could be retained without probable cause be determined, (4) the individual whose information was seized be notified if the information is entered into an electronic database, (5) an individual receive a receipt if his device is seized during a border search, (6) an individual subject to a border search of an electronic device receive notice as to how he can report any abuses or concerns related to the search, (7) the rights of individuals with regard to border searches be posted at all ports of entry, (8) that a privacy impact assessment of the rule be made, and (9) a civil rights impact assessment of the rule be made.

Acknowledgments

This report was originally prepared by Stephen R. Viña. Yule Kim has rewritten and updated the report and is available to answer questions about these issues.

Author Contact Information

Yule Kim
Legislative Attorney
ykim@crs.loc.gov, 7-9138

End Notes

[1] The reasonable suspicion standard requires less suspicion of wrongdoing than probable cause, the normal standard required for a Fourth Amendment search or seizure. *See* Terry v. Ohio, 392 U.S. 1, 21 (1968).

[2] *See infra* "Non-Routine Searches."

[3] Many of the nation's border security agencies or functions have been transferred to the Department of Homeland Security. *See* P.L. 107-296. When discussing case law, this report uses agency names as used in the case law, even if the agency may no longer have responsibilities at the border.

[4] Act of July 18, 1866, ch. 201, § 3, 14 Stat. 178; R.S. § 3061 (codified at 19 U.S.C. § 482).

[5] 19 U.S.C. § 482.

[6] United States v. Rivera, 595 F.2d 1095 (5th Cir. 1979); United States v. Bilir, 592 F.2d 735 (4th Cir. 1979).

[7] United States v. Glaziou, 402 F.2d 8 (2d Cir. 1968); United States v. Berard, 281 F. Supp. 328 (D. Mass. 1968).

[8] United States v. Montoya de Hernandez, 473 U.S. 53, 539 (1985) ("Having presented herself at the border for admission, and having subjected herself to the criminal enforcement powers of the Federal Government, respondent was entitled to be free from unreasonable search and seizure."). *See also* United States v. Bilir, 592 F.2d 735 (4th Cir. 1979); United States v. Bowman, 502 F.2d 1215 (1974).

[9] Normally, reasonable cause is synonymous with probable cause. *See* Black's Law Dictionary 1219 (7th Ed. 1999). However, the Supreme Court interpreted "reasonable cause to suspect" to be a less stringent requirement than probable cause. United States v. Ramsey, 431 U.S. 606, 6 12-13 (1977). Thus, in this context, "reasonable cause to suspect" is more likely equivalent to "reasonable suspicion."

[10] 19 U.S.C. § 482(a).

[11] *Ramsey*, 431 U.S. 606.

[12] *Id.* at 612-13.

[13] *Id.* at 619.

[14] Although the statute speaks of "immigration officers," the Department of Homeland Security (DHS) designates by regulation those classes of DHS agents who actually wield these powers. *See* 8 C.F.R. § 287.5 for a list of officers who are authorized to wield the powers described in this section. Typically, both Border Patrol agents and Immigration and Customs Enforcement agents are empowered to wield all of these powers.

[15] INA § 287(a)(1), 8 U.S.C. § 1357(a)(1) (authorizing any officer or employee "to interrogate any alien or person believed to be an alien as to his right to be or remain in the United States" without obtaining a warrant). *See also* 8 C.F.R. § 287.5 (authorizing all immigration officers to exercise this power).

[16] INA § 287(a)(3), 8 U.S.C. § 1357(a)(3). This statute also authorizes searches without warrant "within a reasonable distance from any external boundary of the United States." *Reasonable distance* is defined by 8 C.F.R. § 287. 1(a)(2) to mean "within 100 air miles from any

external boundary of the United States or any shorter distance which may be fixed by the chief patrol agent of CBP, or the special agent in charge of ICE." *External boundary* is defined by 8 C.F.R. § 287. 1(a)(1) to mean "the land boundaries and the territorial sea of the United States extending 12 nautical miles from the baselines of the United States determined in accordance with international law."

[17] *Id.*

[18] INA § 287(c), 8 U.S.C. § 1357(c).

[19] INA § 287(a)(2), 8 U.S.C. § 1357(a)(2) (authorizing any officer or employee "to arrest any alien who in [the officer's] presence or view is entering or attempting to enter the United States in violation of any law or regulation made in pursuance of law regulating the admission, exclusion, expulsion, or removal of aliens" or "arrest any alien in the United States, if [the officer] has reason to believe that the alien so arrested is in the United States in violation of any such law or regulation and is likely to escape before a warrant can be obtained for his arrest").

[20] *Id.*

[21] INA § 287(a)(4), 8 U.S.C. § 1357(a)(4) (authorizing any officer or employee "to make arrests for felonies which have been committed and which are cognizable under any law of the United States regulating the admission, exclusion, expulsion or removal of aliens, if he has reason to believe that the person so arrested is guilty of such felony and if there is likelihood of the person escaping before a warrant can be obtained for his arrest").

[22] INA § 287(a)(5)(A), 8 U.S.C. § 1357(a)(5)(A).

[23] INA § 287(a)(5)(B), 8 U.S.C. § 1357(a)(5)(B). *See also* 8 C.F.R. § 287.5(c)(4).

[24] *See* Zepeda v. INS, 753 F.2d. 719, 725-26 (9th Cir. 1983) (agreeing with the government's argument that § 287 authorized the interrogation of aliens under the fullest extent permissible under the Fourth Amendment). *See also* Babula v. INS, 665 F.2d 293 (3d Cir. 1981).

[25] United States v. Brignoni-Ponce, 422 U.S. 873 (1975). *See also* United States v. Rogers, 436 F. Supp. 1 (E.D. Mich. 1976) (holding that the Fourth Amendment prohibits identification stops by roving patrols that are not based on articulable suspicion of illegal activity); Illinois Migrant Council v. Pilliod, 531 F. Supp. 1011 (N.D. Ill. 1982) (holding that the Fourth Amendment prohibits INS from conducting investigatory seizures based only on reasonable suspicion that a person seized is an alien).

[26] U.S. Const., Amend. IV.

[27] Katz v. United States, 389 U.S. 347, 357 (1967) ("[S]earches conducted outside the judicial process without prior approval by judge or magistrate are *per se* unreasonable under the Fourth Amendment—subject only to a few specifically established and well delineated exceptions.").

[28] Camara v. Municipal Court, 387 U.S. 523, 539-540 (1967).

[29] *See* Walter v. United States, 447 U.S. 649, 656 (1980) (noting that a wrongful search or seizure conducted by a private party does not violate the Fourth Amendment).

[30] *Katz*, 389 U.S. at 361 (Harlan, J., concurring). *See also* Oliver v. United States, 466 U.S. 170, 177-78 (1984).

[31] Minnesota v. Carter, 525 U.S. 83, 88 (1998).

[32] Kyllo v. United States, 533 U.S. 27, 40 (2001).

[33] Sodal v. Cook County, 506 U.S. 56, 61 (1992) *quoting* United States v. Jacobsen, 466 U.S. 109, 113 (1984).

[34] Florida v. Bostick, 501 U.S. 429, 437 (1991) *citing* Michigan v. Chesternut, 486 U.S. 567, 573 (1988). *See also* United States v. Mendenhall, 446 U.S. 544 (1980); Brendlin v. California, 551 U.S. 249 (2007).

[35] INS v. Delgado, 466 U.S. 210, 216 (1984). *See also* Florida v. Royer, 460 U.S. 491 (1983) ("Interrogation relating to one's identity or a request for identification by the police does not, by itself, constitute a Fourth Amendment seizure.").

[36] *Delgado*, 466 U.S. at 216.

[37] *Id.*; United States v. Rodriguez-Franco, 749 F.2d 1555, 1560 (11th Cir. 1985). *See also* 8 C.F.R. § 287.8(b)(1) ("An immigration officer, like any other person, has the right to ask questions of anyone as long as the immigration officer does not restrain the freedom of an individual, not under arrest, to walk away.").

[38] *Zepeda*, 753 F.2d at 731. *See also* Cuevas-Ortega v. INS, 588 F.2d 1274 (9th Cir. 1979); Cordon de Ruano v. INS, 588 F.2d 1274 (9th Cir. 1977).

[39] *Delgado*, 466 U.S. at 216. *See also Zepeda*, 753 F.2d at 730.

[40] 8 C.F.R. § 287.8(b)(2).

[41] INS v. Lopez-Mendoza, 468 U.S. 1032, 1046 (1984). *See also* Mapp v. Ohio, 367 U.S. 643, 648 (1961) (exclusionary rule in general). *But see* Almeida-Amaral v. Gonzales, 461 F.3d 231, 234 (2d Cir. 2006) ("The [Supreme] Court qualified [*Lopez-Mendoza*]'s ruling in two significant ways. First, it stated that its 'conclusions concerning the exclusionary rule's value might change, if there developed good reason to believe that Fourth Amendment violations by [immigration] officers were widespread.' And, second, it explained that its holding did not necessarily pertain to circumstances involving 'egregious violations of Fourth Amendment or other liberties that might transgress notions of fundamental fairness and undermine the probative value of the evidence obtained.'").

[42] *See supra* "Statutory Authorization to Conduct Border Searches."

[43] Act of July 31, 1789, ch.5 §§ 23-24, 1 Stat. 29, 43 (current version at 19 U.S.C. §§ 482, 1582).

[44] United States v. Ramsey, 431 U.S. 606, 619 (1977) (*citing* U.S. Const., Art. I, § 8, cl. 3).

[45] *See Ramsey*, 431 U.S. at 616.

[46] Marsh v. United States, 344 F.2d 317, 324 (5th Cir. 1965).

[47] United States v. Flores-Montano, 541 U.S. 149 (2004). *See infra* "Searches and Seizures of Vehicles."

[48] Thirty-First Annual Review of Criminal Procedure; Border Searches, 90 Geo. L.J. 1087, 1190 (2002) (9th Cir. 1973).

[49] Almeida-Sanchez v. United States, 413 U.S. 266, 272-73 (1973).

[50] *See* United States v. Hill, 939 F.2d 934, 936 (1 1th Cir. 1991).

[51] *Id.* at 937.

[52] *Id.* at 936 ("Because people can enter the country at points other than along the actual border, courts look to whether the point of entry is the functional equivalent of the border. Places such as international airports within the country and ports within the country's territorial waters exemplify such functional equivalents.").

[53] *Reasonable certainty*, in the context of this test, has been defined as a standard which requires more than probable cause, but less than proof beyond a reasonable doubt. United States v. Cardenas, 9 F.3d 1139, 1148 (5th Cir. 1993).

[54] See, *e.g.*, United States v. Delgado 810 F.2d 480, 482 (5th Cir. 1987). In *Delgado*, smugglers used a foot-bridge to transfer narcotics to delivery trucks on a farm near El Paso, Texas. The court upheld an extended border search conducted on a farm road near and leading from the border, but not at the official border checkpoint.

[55] United States v. Teng Yang, 286 F.3d. 940, 946 (7th Cir. 2002).

[56] *See, e.g., Teng Yang*, 286 F.3d. 940; United States v. Sahanaja, 430 F.3d 1049 (9th Cir. 2005); United States v. Espinoza-Seanez, 862 F.2d 526 (5th Cir. 1989); United States v. Caicedo-Guarnizo, 723 F.2d 1420 (9th Cir. 1984); United States v. Garcia, 672 F.2d 1349 (1 1th Cir. 1982); United States v. Bilir, 592 F.2d 735 (4th Cir. 1979).

[57] United States v. Niver, 689 F.2d 520, 526 (5th Cir. 1982).

[58] 286 F.3d. 940 (7th Cir. 2002).

[59] *Id.* at 947.

[60] *See, e.g.*, 8 U.S.C. § 1357(c) (authorizing immigration officials to search without a warrant persons entering the country for evidence which may lead to the individual's exclusion); 19 U.S.C. § 1496 (authorizing customs officials to search the baggage of person entering the country); 19 U.S.C. § 1582 (authorizing customs officials to detain and search all persons

coming into the United States from foreign countries). *See also* United States v. Montoya de Hernandez, 473 U.S. 531, 538 (1985).

[61] United States v. Johnson, 991 F.2d 1287, 1291 (7th Cir. 1993).

[62] *See, e.g.*, United States v. Beras, 183 F.3d 22, 24 (1st Cir. 1999) (holding that a patdown of an international traveler's legs was not intrusive enough to qualify as non-routine).

[63] United States v. Sandler, 644 F.2d 1163, 1169 (5th Cir. 1981).

[64] United States v. Kelly, 302 F.3d 291, 294-95 (5th Cir. 2002) (sniff by a dog of a person at the border upheld as a routine border search); *cf. United States v. Garcia-Garcia*, 319 F.3d 726, 730 (5th Cir. 2003) (dog sniff of a person on a bus at an immigration checkpoint upheld and seen as analogous to a pat down).

[65] United States v. Kolawole Odutayo, 406 F.3d 386, 392 (5th Cir. 2005) (joining sister circuits in holding that the border search exception applies for all outgoing searches at the border).

[66] United States v. Okafor, 285 F.3d 842 (9th Cir. 2002) (finding an X-ray examination and subsequent probe of luggage a routine search because it requires no force, poses no risk to the bag's owner or to the public, causes no psychological fear, and does not harm the baggage); United States v. Lawson, 461 F.3d 697, 701 (6th Cir. 2006) (accepting the "commonsense conclusion that customs officers may x-ray an airline passenger's luggage at the border without reasonable suspicion").

[67] Gary N. Jacobs, Note, *Border Searches and the Fourth Amendment*, 77 Yale L.J. 1007, 1012 (1968). It should also be noted that the "reasonable person" test presupposes an innocent person who has nothing to conceal from customs. *Bostick*, 501 U.S. at 437.

[68] United States v. Odland, 502 F.2d 148 (7th Cir. 1974) *citing* Carroll v. United States, 267 U.S. 132, 153 (1925). Some courts have indicated a need for "mere suspicion" to conduct a routine border search, which usually requires at least some knowledge identifying an individual as a suspect. *See, e.g.*, Rodriguez-Gonzalez v. United States, 378 F.2d 256 (9th Cir. 1967) (also using the term *unsupported suspicion*). This standard, however, is an inaccurate articulation of the general rule that no suspicion is required. *See Odland*, 502 F.2d at 151 ("Any person or thing coming into the United States is subject to search by that fact alone, whether or not there be any suspicion of illegality directed to the particular person or thing to be searched."); Bradley v. United States, 299 F.3d 197, n.7 (3d Cir. 2002) (stating "mere suspicion" standard effectively overruled by *Montoya de Hernandez*).

[69] 77 Yale L.J. 1007, 1012 (1968).

[70] United States v. Braks, 842 F.2d 509, 511-12 (1st Cir. 1988). The *Braks* court concluded that only strip searches and body cavity searches are consistently non-routine.

[71] *See, e.g.*, United States v. Reyes, 821 F.2d 168, 170-71 (2d Cir. 1987) (strip search); United States v. Oyekan, 786 F.2d 832, 837 (8th Cir. 1986) (strip search); United States v. Adekunle, 2 F.3d 559, 562 (5th Cir. 1993) (continued detention and X-ray examination of alimentary canal); United States v. Rivas, 157 F.3d 364, 367 (5th Cir. 1998) (drilling of hole into body of automobile).

[72] *Montoya de Hernandez*, 473 U.S. at 541; United States v. Garcia-Garcia, 319 F.3d 726, 730 (5th Cir. 2003) (an alert by a drug sniffing dog provided reasonable suspicion to detain a bus long enough to investigate the reason for the dog's response).

[73] *See Montoya de Hernandez*, 473 U.S. at 541 *citing Terry,* 392 U.S. at 21 ("And in justifying the particular intrusion the police officer must be able to point to specific and articulable facts which, taken together with rational inferences from those facts, reasonably warrant that intrusion.").

[74] 484 F.2d 645 (5th Cir. 1973). *But see* Reid v. Georgia, 448 U.S. 438, 441(1980) (rejecting the argument that arrival from a source location could, by itself, provide reasonable suspicion).

[75] See *Montoya de Hernandez*, 473 U.S. at 541 n.4.

[76] *Id.* at 541.

[77] *Id.* at 540.

[78] *See, e.g.*, United States v. Charleus, 871 F.2d 265, 268 n.2 (2d Cir. 1989); United States v. Oyekan, 786 F.2d 832, 837-39 (8th Cir. 1986); *Bradley v. United States*, 299 F.3d 197, 202-

04 (3[d] Cir. 2002). United States v. Aguebor, 1999 U.S. App. Lexis 25, at *9 (4th Cir. January 4, 1999) (This unpublished opinion is cited merely as an example and is not intended to have precedential value.).

[79] *See, e.g.*, United States v. Ramos-Saenz, 36 F.3d 59, 61 (9th Cir. 1994) (requiring the higher "clear indication" standard for a body cavity search); United States v. Ek, 676 F.2d 379, 382 (9th Cir. 1982) (requiring a "clear indication" for X-ray search).

[80] *Montoya de Hernandez*, 473 U.S. at 541. *See also* United States v. Esieke, 940 F.2d 29 (2[d] Cir. 1991) (court upheld a detention of one and half days before first bowel movement and another two and half days until all balloons were expelled); United States v. Yakubu, 936 F.2d 936 (7th Cir. 1991) (16-hour detention upheld after refusal to be X-rayed).

[81] *Montoya de Hernandez* does not stand for a "detention until defecation" proposition. The court narrowly decided that the particular detention "was not unreasonably long" under "these circumstances." In fact, the agents expected Ms. Montoya de Hernandez to produce a bowel movement without extended delay because she had just disembarked from a 10-hour flight. 4 Wayne R. LaFave, Search and Seizure, A Treatise on the Fourth Amendment § 10.5(b), 546 (3[d] ed. 1996 & Supp. 2003).

[82] *Esieke*, 940 F.2d at 35.

[83] 2 F.3d 559, 562 (5th Cir. 1993). The court opined that a formal determination is not necessary; rather, an informal presentation of the evidence supporting the government's suspicion before a neutral and detached judicial officer satisfies this requirement. Furthermore, the court concluded that the failure to obtain such a judicial determination within 48 hours shifts the burden to the government to demonstrate a *bona fide* emergency justifying the extended detainment.

[84] *See* Tabbaa v. Chertoff, 509 F.3d 89, 99 (2[d] Cir. 2007) (*quoting Montoya de Hernandez*, 473 U.S. at 543).

[85] *Tabbaa*, 509 F.3d at 99.

[86] *Montoya de Hernandez*, 473 U.S. at 535.

[87] *Flores-Montano*, 541 U.S. at 151.

[88] *Tabbaa,* 509 F.3d at 99.

[89] United States v. Chase, 503 F.2d 571 (9th Cir. 1974).

[90] 477 F.2d 608 (1st Cir. 1973).

[91] *Id.*

[92] *See, e.g.*, United States v. Ogberaha, 771 F.2d 655, 657 (2[d] Cir. 1985) (vagina); United States v. Pino, 729 F.2d 1357, 1358 (11th Cir. 1984) (rectum); United States v. Briones, 423 F.2d 742, 743 (5th Cir. 1970) (emetics).

[93] *See, e.g.*, United States v. Sosa, 469 F.2d 271 (9th Cir. 1972) (no warrant for rectal probe); United States v. Mason, 480 F.2d 563 (9th Cir. 1973) (no warrant for vaginal probe); United States v. Briones, 423 F.2d 742 (5th Cir. 1970) (no warrant for administration of an emetic). *But see* United States v. Holtz, 479 F.2d 89 (9th Cir. 1973) (Ely, J., dissenting); Blefare v. United States, 362 F.2d 870 (9th Cir. 1966) (Ely, J., dissenting).

[94] *See, e.g.*, United States v. Ogberaha, 771 F.2d 658 (2[d] Cir. 1985); Swain v. Spinney, 117 F.3d 1, 7 (1st Cir. 1997) (only required reasonable suspicion for visual body cavity search); United States v. Gonzalez-Ricon, 36 F.3d 859, 864 (9th Cir. 1984) (noting in dictum that a body cavity search must be supported by reasonable suspicion). Due to the intrusiveness of alimentary canal searches, some courts had required a "clear indication" (a suggestion that is free from doubt) of alimentary canal smuggling to justify the search. *See, e.g.*, United States v. Ramos-Saenz, 36 F.3d 59, 61 (9th Cir. 1994) (affirming clear indication standard). But since the Supreme Court expressed its disapproval of suspicion standards other than "reasonable suspicion" in *Montoya de Hernandez*, courts have been unwilling to adopt the "clear indication" standard for body cavity searches. *See, e.g.*, United States v. Ogberaha, 771 F.2d 658 (2[d] Cir. 1985); Swain v. Spinney, 117 F.3d 1, 7 (1st Cir. 1997) (only required reasonable suspicion for visual body cavity search); United States v. Bravo, 295 F.3d 1002

(9th Cir. 2002) (noting in dictum that a body cavity search must be supported by reasonable suspicion).

[95] Rochin v. California, 342 U.S. 165 (1952).

[96] *Id.*

[97] Rectal searches have been upheld when conducted by medical personnel using accepted and customary medical techniques in medical surroundings. *See, e.g.,* Rivas v. United States, 368 F.2d 703 (9th Cir. 1966) (upholding rectal search by a doctor at doctor's office).

[98] United States v. Vega-Barvo, 729 F.2d 1341, 1345-46 (11th Cir. 1984).

[99] *Id.*

[100] *Id.* at 1346.

[101] *Id.* at 1348.

[102] *See supra* "Non-Routine Searches." Although some courts had previously required the more stringent "clear indication" standard for X-ray searches, ever since the Supreme Court denounced "clear indication" in *Montoya de Hernandez,* courts now generally analogize X-rays with strip searches and only require reasonable suspicion. *Compare* United States v. Ek, 676 F.2d 379, 382 (9th Cir. 1982) (determining that while an X-ray search may not be as humiliating as a strip search, "it is more intrusive since the search is potentially harmful to the health of the suspect") *with* United States v. Oyekan, 786 F.2d 832, 837 (8th Cir. 1986) (requiring reasonable suspicion for X-ray search); United States v. Pino, 729 F.2d 1357, 1359 (11th Cir. 1984) (X-ray search equal to strip search).

[103] 509 F.3d 89, 99 (2d Cir. 2007).

[104] *Id.*

[105] *Id.*

[106] *Id.*

[107] *Id.*

[108] United States v. Flores-Montano, 541 U.S. 149, 152 (2004) ("Complex balancing tests to determine what is a 'routine' search of a vehicle, as opposed to a more 'intrusive' search of a person, have no place in border searches of vehicles.").

[109] *See, e.g.,* United States v. Robles, 45 F.3d 1, 5 (1st Cir. 1995).

[110] *Id.* (drilling a hole into a metal cylinder transported to an airport on an international flight was a non-routine search); United States v. Rivas, 157 F.3d 364, 367 (5th Cir. 1998) (drilling a hole into a tractor-trailer's frame was a non-routine search); United States v. Carreon, 872 F.2d 1436, 1440-41 (10th Cir. 1989) (implicitly requiring that drilling a hole into a camper wall in order to effect a search of its interior required reasonable suspicion to be justified).

[111] *Id.* at 152-53 *quoting Ramsey,* 431 U.S. at 616.

[112] *Id.* at 153.

[113] *Id.* at 155, n.2 (*citing Rivas,* 157 F.3d 364 (5th Cir. 1998) (drilling into body of trailer required reasonable suspicion); United States v. Robles, 45 F.3d 1 (1st Cir. 1995) (drilling into machine part required reasonable suspicion); *United States v. Carreon,* 872 F.2d 1436 (10th Cir. 1989) (drilling into camper required reasonable suspicion).

[114] *Flores-Montano,* 541 U.S. at 155-156.

[115] *Id.* at 155, n.2.

[116] *Flores-Montano,* 541 U.S. at 155-156; United States v. Bennett, 363 F.3d 947, 951 (9th Cir. 2004). *Cf. Okafor,* 285 F.3d at 846 (qualifying its holding by stating that a suspicionless X-ray search of luggage may be done at the border "[s]o long as the means of examination are not personally intrusive, do not significantly harm the objects scrutinized, and do not unduly delay transit").

[117] United States v. Cortez-Rocha, 394 F.3d 1115, 1119 (9th Cir. 2005).

[118] *Flores-Montano,* 424 F.3d at 1049, n.6 (This case dealt with the same defendant as the Supreme Court case but posed a different legal question.). *See also Cortez-Rocha,* 394 F.3d at 1119; United States v. Chaudhry, 424 F.3d 1051, 1054 (9th Cir. 2005).

[119] *Cortez-Rocha,* 394 F.3d 1115.

[120] *Id.* at 1119-1120.

[121] United States v. Chaudhry, 424 F.3d 1051, 1053 (9th Cir. 2005).

[122] United States v. Camacho, 368 F.3d 1182 (9th Cir. 2004). The Ninth Circuit in this case distinguished prior precedent (*Ek*, 676 F.2d 379) requiring a heightened level of suspicion for X-ray searches of persons because such searches were potentially harmful to the health of the suspect, whereas the "Buster" search was not harmful to motorists.

[123] United States v. Hernandez, 424 F.3d 1056 (9th Cir. 2005).

[124] *Chaudhry*, 424 F.3d at 1054-1055 (Fletcher, J., concurring) ("In each case, the government chose to create a dispute where none existed, rather than to prove up its officers' valid suspicions."); (Fisher, J. concurring) ("I am troubled by the government's evident decision in this and other cases to eschew reliance on dog alerts or other evidence supporting reasonable suspicion.") *Id.* at 1055.

[125] *See* CRS Report RL34404, *Border Searches of Laptop Computers and Other Electronic Storage Devices*, by Yule Kim, Border Searches of Laptop Computers and Other Electronic Storage Devices, by Yule Kim for an in-depth analysis of this issue.

[126] *See, e.g.*, United States v. Ickes, 393 F.3d 501, 505 (4th Cir. 2005); United States v. Romm, 455 F.3d 990, 997 (9th Cir. 2006); United States v. Irving, 452 F.3d 110, 123 (2d Cir. 2006); United States v. Furukawa, No. 06-145, slip op. (D. Minn., November 16, 2006), 2006 U.S. Dist. LEXIS 83767; United States v. Hampe, No. 07-3-B-W, slip op. (D. Me., April 18, 2007), 2007 U.S. Dist. LEXIS 29218.

[127] *See, e.g.*, *Irving*, 452 F.3d at 124 ("Because these searches were supported by reasonable suspicion, we need not determine whether they were routine or non-routine."); *Furukawa*, *supra* ("[T]he court need not determine whether a border search of a laptop is 'routine' for purposes of the Fourth Amendment because, regardless, the magistrate judge correctly found the customs official had a reasonable suspicion in this case.").

[128] *Ickes*, 393 F.3d at 507 (noting that the computer search did not begin until the custom agents found marijuana paraphernalia and child pornography which raised a reasonable suspicion); *Hampe*, *supra* (holding that even though the laptop search did not implicate any of the serious concerns that would characterize a search as non-routine, that the peculiar facts of the case gave rise to reasonable suspicions).

[129] United States v. Arnold, 533 F.3d 1003 (9th Cir. 2008).

[130] *Id.* at 1008.

[131] *Id.* at 1007.

[132] *Id.*

[133] *Id.* at 1007-08.

[134] *Id.* at 1009-10.

[135] As a side note, even though these cases usually arise in child pornography prosecutions, there are national security implications involved as well. For example, one of the justifications given for not requiring probable cause to conduct a laptop search is that to do so would enable terrorists to smuggle potentially incriminating information on electronic media without fear of it being searched. *Ickes*, 393 F.3d at 506. Another potential issue that might arise is the possibility that the search power could be abused if an officer does not need to provide an articulable reason for his search.

[136] *Id.* at 507-08.

[137] *Id.* at 506-07 *citing* New York v. P.J. Video, 475 U.S. 868, 874 (1986). *See also* United States v. 37 Photographs, 402 U.S. 363, 376 (1974) (finding that particularized suspicion not required for searches of pictures, films and other graphic materials); United States v. 12,200 Feet Reels of Super 8mm Film, 413 U.S. 128, 124-25 (1973).

[138] *Arnold*, 533 F.3d at 1010.

[139] 547 F.3d 993, 996 (9th Cir. 2008).

[140] *Id.* at 996 (*citing* 31 U.S.C. § 5317(b)).

[141] *Id.* at 1003.

[142] *Id.* at 1004.

[143] *Id.* at 1014 (Kozinski, J., dissenting).

[144] *Id.* at 1017-19 (Kozinski, J., dissenting).

[145] *Id.* at 1017 (Kozinksi, J., dissenting) (*citing Entick v. Harrington*, 19 Howell's State Trials 1029, 95 Eng. Rep. 807 (1765)).

[146] *Id.* (Kozinski, J., dissenting).

[147] *Id.* at 1016. (Kozinski, J., dissenting).

[148] *Id.* at 1014-15 (Kozinski, J., dissenting).

[149] The 9/11 Commission Report: Final Report on the National Commission on Terrorist Attacks Upon the United States, p. 385 (Official Gov't Ed. 2004).

[150] *Id.* at 385-390.

[151] Implementing Recommendations of 9/11 Commission Act of 2007, P.L. 110-53, 121 Stat. 266.

In: The Fourth Amendment
Editors: Jesse V. Kessler

ISBN: 978-1-61728-885-2

Chapter 2

BORDER SEARCHES OF LAPTOP COMPUTERS AND OTHER ELECTRONIC STORAGE DEVICES

Yule Kim

SUMMARY

As a general rule, the Fourth Amendment of the U.S. Constitution requires government-conducted searches and seizures to be supported by probable cause and a warrant. Federal courts have long recognized that there are many exceptions to these requirements, one of which is the border search exception. The border search exception permits government officials to conduct "routine" searches based on no suspicion of wrongdoing whatsoever. On the other hand, when warrantless border searches are particularly invasive, and thus "non-routine," they are permissible only when customs officials have, at a minimum, a "reasonable suspicion" of wrongdoing.

The federal courts that have addressed this issue have held that the border search exception applies to searches of laptops at the border. Although the Supreme Court has not directly addressed the degree of suspicion needed to search laptops at the border without a warrant, the federal appellate courts that have addressed the issue appear to have concluded that reasonable suspicion is not needed to justify such a search. The Ninth Circuit, in *United States v.*

Arnold, explicitly held that reasonable suspicion is not required to conduct a warrantless search of a laptop at the border.

Customs and Border Protection (CBP) and Immigration and Customs Enforcement (ICE), two agencies within the Department of Homeland Security (DHS) that have roles in border security, have published directives outlining their policies and procedures regarding laptop border searches. Both policies assert that, as a general matter, laptop border searches may be conducted without any individualized suspicion and require reasonable suspicion only in certain circumstances.

A bill introduced in the 111th Congress, the Securing our Borders and our Data Act of 2009 (H.R. 239), would impose more rigorous standards for laptop searches than those the federal courts have determined are constitutionally required. Another bill introduced in the 111th Congress, the Border Security Search Accountability Act of 2009 (H.R. 1726), would mandate that the Commissioner of Customs and Border Protection promulgate a rule with respect to the scope of and procedural and record keeping requirements associated with border security searches of electronic devices.

Introduction

A developing issue in the law of search and seizure is whether the Fourth Amendment of the U.S. Constitution permits warrantless searches of the content of laptop computers and other electronic storage devices at U.S. borders. The federal courts that have addressed this issue have held that the border search exception to the Fourth Amendment applies to these searches, making warrantless searches permissible. Although most of these courts did not make explicit the degree of suspicion needed to initiate such a search, the United States Court of Appeals for the Ninth Circuit ruled that the Fourth Amendment does not require reasonable suspicion, or, for that matter, any suspicion of wrongdoing at all, to justify a warrantless search of laptops at the border.

Border Search Exception

The Fourth Amendment mandates that a search or seizure conducted by a government agent must be "reasonable."[1] As a general rule, courts have construed Fourth Amendment *reasonableness* as requiring probable cause[2] and a judicially granted warrant.[3] Nonetheless, the Supreme Court has recognized several exceptions to these requirements, one of which is the border search exception.[4]

The border search exception to the Fourth Amendment allows federal government officials to conduct searches at the border without a warrant or probable cause. Although Congress and the federal courts have long assumed, at least implicitly, the existence of a border search exception,[5] the Supreme Court did not formally recognize it until it decided *Ramsey v. United States* in 1977.[6] In *Ramsey*, the Supreme Court approved the search of several suspicious envelopes (later found to contain heroin) conducted by a customs official pursuant to search powers authorized by statute.[7] The Court determined that the customs official had "reasonable cause to suspect"[8] suspicious activity when searching the envelopes.[9] This standard, while less stringent than probable cause, was sufficient justification.[10] The border search exception has subsequently been expanded beyond persons, objects, and mail entering the United States, to cover individuals and objects departing from the United States[11] and to apply in places deemed the "functional equivalent" of a border, such as international airports.[12]

As the border search exception has further developed in case law, lower federal courts have recognized two different categories of border searches: routine and non-routine. This distinction is based on language in *United States v. Montoya de Hernandez*, where the Supreme Court determined the level of suspicion needed to justify "a seizure of an incoming traveler for purposes other than a routine border search."[13] In that case, customs officials detained a traveler whom they suspected of smuggling drugs.[14] The customs officials eventually obtained a court order authorizing a rectal examination, which produced a balloon containing cocaine.[15] The Court held that, even though the detention "was beyond the scope of a routine customs search and inspection," the customs officials' "reasonable suspicion" that the suspect was smuggling drugs provided sufficient justification for the search.[16] Federal courts have since interpreted this case to stand for the proposition that "reasonable suspicion" (i.e., a particularized and objective basis for suspecting wrongdoing) is required to justify similarly invasive searches.[17]

Although the Court in *Montoya de Hernandez* focused on a "non-routine" detention of a traveler at the border, lower federal courts, interpreting *dictum* in that case, began distinguishing unusually intrusive searches from "routine" searches.[18] These courts thereby expanded the border search exception by concluding that a customs official may conduct "routine" warrantless searches of persons or effects without any reason for suspicion. [19] The Supreme Court further developed this doctrine in *United States v. Flores-Montano*, in which it held that the disassembly and examination of an automobile gasoline tank at the border did not have to be justified by any suspicion of wrongdoing.[20] The Court concluded that the gasoline tank search was no more intrusive than a routine vehicle search because there was no heightened expectation of privacy surrounding the contents of a gasoline tank; this conclusion was reached even though the search involved a time-consuming disassembly of the vehicle.[21] *Flores-Montano* illustrates that extensive, time-consuming, and potentially destructive warrantless searches of objects and effects can be conducted without any reasonable suspicion of wrongdoing.

In summary, Supreme Court precedent currently indicates that federal border officers do not need any suspicion of wrongdoing to support most border searches. An exception arises, however, with respect to highly intrusive, non-routine searches. These searches require "reasonable suspicion."[22] Yet, the precise level of intrusion that would render a border search non-routine is undefined in the case law.[23] Typically, this question is dealt with in a fact-specific manner on a case-by-case basis.[24] Nonetheless, *Flores-Montano* indicates that, unlike a search of a person's body, intrusiveness may not be a dispositive factor when determining whether the search of a vehicle or personal effects requires reasonable suspicion. Thus, it appears that in most cases, courts are likely to uphold that even very invasive searches of personal property can be conducted without a warrant and be based on no suspicion whatsoever.[25]

Judicial Developments on Laptop Searches

With the advent of portable computing, it is now common practice for travelers to store their data on laptop computers, compact discs, and other electronic storage devices and to travel with them across the U.S. border. In response, customs officials have been searching and seizing such devices. The issue confronting federal courts is whether the border search exception applies to electronic storage devices, and if it does, what degree of suspicion is needed to justify a warrantless search.

The Supreme Court has yet to address this issue. Most lower federal courts, however, have concluded that searches of laptops, computer disks, and other electronic storage devices fall under the border search exception, which means neither a warrant nor probable cause is necessary to support the search.[26] Nonetheless, these courts have not explicitly established the degree of suspicion required to justify a warrantless search of a laptop at the border; rather, courts have avoided the issue by finding that reasonable suspicion supported the particular searches before them.[27] Even in the one instance a court held that a laptop search was routine, it also found that reasonable suspicion supported the search.[28] The one exception to this trend is *United States v. Arnold*, in which the Ninth Circuit explicitly held that reasonable suspicion was not needed to support a warrantless border search of laptops and other electronic storage devices.[29] Because laptop border search cases are a developing area of case law, a full understanding of this issue requires a closer look at the facts of these cases and the approaches the courts used in their analyses.

United States v. Ickes

One of the first federal appellate cases to discuss searches of laptops at the border is *United States v. Ickes*.[30] In *Ickes*, a customs official, without a warrant, searched the defendant's van near the Canadian border after discovering during a routine search a videotape that focused excessively on a young ballboy during a tennis match.[31] His suspicions raised, the official requested the assistance of a colleague. They then proceeded to conduct a more thorough search in which they uncovered marijuana paraphernalia, a photo album containing child pornography, a computer, and several computer disks.[32] Other customs officials proceeded to examine the contents of the computer and disks, all of which contained additional child pornography.[33] The defendant later filed a motion, which was denied by the trial court, seeking to suppress the contents of the computer and disks on both First and Fourth Amendment grounds.[34]

The Fourth Circuit held that the search of the defendant's computer and disks did not violate either the Fourth or First Amendment. Regarding the Fourth Amendment challenge, the court noted that the border search exception applied in this case.[35] The court concluded by opining that "[a]s a practical matter, computer searches are most likely to occur where—as here—the traveler's conduct or the presence of other items in his possession suggest the need to search further," indicating that the court believed that such searches will typically occur only when a customs official has reasonable suspicion.[36]

The court also rejected the defendant's contention that the First Amendment bars the border search exception from being applied to "expressive" materials. The court stated that a First Amendment exception would "create a sanctuary for all expressive materials—including terrorist plans," and that it would cause an excessive amount of administrative difficulties for those who would have to enforce it.[37]

United States v. Romm

The Ninth Circuit has also addressed this issue in *United States v. Romm*.[38] The defendant in that case had arrived at an airport in British Columbia when a Canadian customs agent, after discovering that he had a criminal history, searched the defendant's laptop.[39] During the search, the Canadian customs agent uncovered child pornography sites in the laptop's "internet history"; the defendant was consequently denied entry into Canada and flown to Seattle.[40] The Canadian authorities informed U.S. Immigration and Customs Enforcement (ICE) of the contents of the defendant's laptop. When the defendant arrived in Seattle, ICE detained the defendant and convinced him to allow ICE agents to examine his laptop without a warrant.[41] ICE agents then used a forensic analysis, which recovered deleted child pornography from the laptop. The defendant later filed a motion to suppress the evidence obtained from his laptop, which the trial court denied.[42]

The Ninth Circuit held that the forensic analysis used by the ICE agents fell under the border search exception.[43] The court noted that airport terminals were "the functional equivalents" of a border, allowing customs agents to conduct routine border searches of all deplaning passengers.[44] The court then stated that all passengers deplaning from an international flight are subject to "routine" border searches.[45] Because the defendant failed to brief the argument that the First Amendment implications of warrantless laptop searches render such searches "non-routine," the court did not consider that argument.[46] The court instead presumed that the search of the defendant's laptop was a part of a "routine" search conducted after deplaning from an international flight.[47] However, because the court made this conclusion solely because the defendant failed to brief his argument, the court's determination that the search was "routine" had no precedential effect.[48]

United States v. Arnold

In *United States v. Arnold*, another Ninth Circuit case, the court, apparently disregarding the traditional routine/non-routine distinction used in most border search cases, expressly held that reasonable suspicion was not required to support the warrantless laptop border search at issue.[49] Here, the defendant had returned from the Philippines when he underwent secondary questioning at the airport after having passed through the first customs checkpoint.[50] The customs agent, without a warrant, ordered the defendant to "turn on the computer so she could see if it was functioning."[51] While the defendant's luggage was being inspected, another customs agent searched the laptop's contents and found pictures of nude adult women. [52] The defendant was then detained for several hours while special agents from ICE conducted a more extensive search of the laptop and discovered material they believed to be child pornography.[53]

The Ninth Circuit first stated that warrantless "searches of closed containers and their contents can be conducted at the border without particularized suspicion under the Fourth Amendment."[54] Nonetheless, the court noted that the Supreme Court has recognized two situations where reasonable suspicion is required to conduct a search of personal property: (1) when the search is destructive, and (2) when the search is conducted in a particularly offensive manner.[55] Outside of these two situations, reasonable suspicion is not required to search property, regardless of the nature of the property being searched. Thus, the Ninth Circuit refused to take into consideration any special qualities of laptops that may distinguish them from other containers, such as a laptop's capability of storing large amounts of private data. Indeed, the court did not find the search of a laptop to be intrinsically "offensive" simply because a laptop had a large storage capacity.[56] Instead, the court treated border searches of laptops no differently from border searches of any other type of personal property.[57]

The Ninth Circuit, in its analysis, rejected the use of an "intrusiveness analysis." An intrusiveness analysis would require a customs officer to evaluate the potential intrusiveness of each search he wished to conduct on a case-by-case basis in order to determine whether reasonable suspicion would be needed to justify the search.[58] The court instead adopted a categorical approach to warrantless border searches: so long as the search is of a physical object rather than a person's body, reasonable suspicion is not required if the search is not physically destructive or particularly offensive.

The Ninth Circuit also refused to apply a "least restrictive means" test to evaluate the constitutionality of a border agent's chosen method of conducting the search.[59] Thus, under the court's analysis, a border agent seemingly can conduct a search without having to determine whether a less intrusive means is available. The argument in favor of this categorical approach is that it appears easier for border agents to follow. On the other hand, the breadth of the Ninth Circuit's ruling apparently allows border agents, so long as they avoid searching a person's body, almost total discretion in determining both when, and in what manner, they may search personal property.

Finally, the Ninth Circuit refused to recognize a First Amendment protection of expressive materials searched at the border. Similar to the reasoning in *Ickes*, the court held that doing so could protect terrorist communications, create an unworkable standard for government agents, and contravene Supreme Court precedent.[60]

United States v. Seljan

The majority opinion in *United States v. Seljan* reaffirmed *Arnold* by holding that an incidental search of a letter's content at the border did not require reasonable suspicion.[61] However, a dissent by Judge Alex Kozinski argued that reasonable suspicion was required because a letter contains personal thoughts that the letter's author would expect to be normally immune from search, especially absent suspicion of wrongdoing. Although the facts of this case only involve letters, the analyses of both the majority and dissenting opinions address the search of text, and thus would seem to apply to written communications generally, including electronic communications.

In this case, a customs official discovered a letter soliciting sex from a child while searching a package being mailed to the Philippines. The search of the letter's contents was upheld even though the scope of the statute authorizing the search was limited to the interdiction of undeclared currency transported across the U.S. border.[62] Indeed, the *Seljan* majority specifically cited *Ramsey*, arguably the seminal case concerning the border search doctrine, in holding that "an envelope containing personal correspondence is not uniquely protected from search at the border."[63] Moreover, the court found additional justification for the search by concluding that it was not unreasonable under the circumstances because the customs official did not "read" the contents of the letter. Rather, he merely "scanned" it with his eyes, which then gave rise to the reasonable suspicion of unlawful conduct that justified a more exacting examination of the letter's contents.[64]

In contrast, Judge Kozinksi, in his dissent, argued that the Fourth Amendment provides heightened protections for expressive materials at the border.[65] He made two arguments to support this proposition. The first is based on the Fourth Amendment's text, which contains a specific prohibition against the unreasonable search and seizure of "papers." Judge Kozinski argued that this specific prohibition signals the Framers' desire to insulate expressive content, and the personal thoughts contained therein, from unnecessary government search.[66] In support of this interpretation, Judge Kozinski cited *Entick v. Carrington*, an English common law case which would have been familiar to the Framers, which rejected "the government's claim of unrestrained power to search personal papers" and held that the searches and seizures of documents violated English common law.[67] According to his analysis, the prevailing view at the time of *Entick* was that a search of private papers was every bit as intrusive as a body search, which, if accurate, would indicate that the Framers intended individualized suspicion to be required to support a search of papers even at the border.[68] Second, Judge Kozinski also distinguished *Seljan* from past Supreme Court precedent by characterizing the border search exception as a means to facilitate the interdiction of smuggled contraband.[69] Thus, according to Judge Kozinski, the border search exception should be limited to the search of "containers," primarily for the purpose of uncovering contraband, and should not be applied to facilitate the search of expressive materials.[70]

FEDERAL POLICIES ON BORDER LAPTOP SEARCHES

Customs and Border Protection (CBP) and Immigration and Customs Enforcement (ICE) have issued directives outlining their policies and procedures regarding the border searches of laptops and other electronic devices. Both CBP and ICE are agencies within the Department of Homeland Security (DHS). CBP provides security at the U.S. borders and ports of entry by inspecting incoming persons and cargo in order to prevent the entry of certain individuals and goods, such as terrorists, unauthorized immigrants, contraband (i.e., illegal narcotics), and agricultural goods contaminated with pests or disease. ICE investigates individuals and criminal networks suspected of facilitating illegal activities such as unauthorized immigration, terrorism, and contraband smuggling.[71] Both directives assert that CBP and ICE do not require any individualized suspicion to search laptops and other electronic devices at the border, and outline similar procedures regarding the handling of seized materials.[72]

Customs and Border Protection Policy

U.S. Customs and Border Protection (CBP), the primary agency entrusted with border security, has released a "Directive" outlining the procedures "all CBP Officers, Border Patrol Agents, Interdiction Agents, Marine Interdiction Agents, and other employees authorized by law to perform searches at the border or the functional equivalent of the border, or the extended border" must follow when conducting border searches of laptops. This Directive, dated August 20, 2009, contains

> [g]uidance and standard operating procedures for searching, reviewing, retaining, and sharing information contained in computers, disks, drives, tapes, mobile phones and other communication devices, cameras, music and other media players, and any other electronic or digital devices, encountered by [CBP] at the border, both inbound and outbound, to ensure compliance with customs, immigration, and other laws that CBP is authorized to enforce.[73]

The Directive is limited to CBP's border search authority, and is not meant to limit CBP's authority to conduct other lawful searches at the border, such as those conducted pursuant to a warrant, consent, or incident to an arrest. It also is not intended to govern searches of commercial quantities of electronic devices (i.e., those transported in a shipping container).[74]

The Directive states that CBP officers may, with or without individualized suspicion, during the course of a border search examine an electronic device and analyze the information it contains. Furthermore, such searches should be conducted in the presence of the individual whose information is being examined unless "there are national security, law enforcement, or other operational considerations" to render the individual's presence during the search inappropriate. However, the Directive contains a caveat that an individual's presence does not necessarily mean the individual can witness the search itself, and an individual will not be allowed to witness the search if "law enforcement techniques or other operational considerations" stand to be compromised.[75]

The Directive also outlines procedures related to the search of privileged or other sensitive materials. Under the directive, legal materials, medical records, journalist work-related information, and business or commercial information may all be subject to search.[76] Legal materials are subject to special handling procedures. Specifically, if a CBP officer encounters legal materials he suspects may constitute evidence of a crime or otherwise pertain to a determination within the jurisdiction of CBP (e.g., customs searches or immigration inspection), the officer must first consult with the CBP Associate/Assistant Chief Counsel before searching the material.[77]

Medical records and journalist work-related information shall be handled in accordance with "any applicable federal law and CBP policy."[78] All business and commercial information encountered by CBP officers shall be treated as confidential and officers shall protect this information from unauthorized disclosures.[79] If a CBP officer has questions related to the review of these categories of information, they may be directed to the CBP Associate/Assistant Chief Counsel.[80]

Detention and review policies are also dictated by the Directive. It states that an officer "may detain electronic devices, or copies of information contained herein, for a brief, reasonable period of time to perform a thorough border search."[81] This search may take place on-site or off-site and should not exceed five days.[82] However, detentions may be extended by five days if approved by a Port Director, Patrol Agent in Charge, or other equivalent-level manager, and they can exceed 15 days if approved by "the Director Field Operations, Chief Patrol Agent, Director, Air Operations, Director, Marine Operations, or other equivalent manager." Thereafter, extensions may be approved and re-approved in increments of seven days.[83] Furthermore, if review of the information reveals there is no probable cause to seize it, all copies of the information must be destroyed no later than seven days after the no probable cause determination is made, unless a supervisor approves an extension, which can last no longer than 21 days.[84]

The Directive also claims the right to use "other federal agency analytical resources outside of CBP and ICE, such as translation, decryption, and subject matter expertise."[85] Technical assistance (i.e., assistance in operating the electronic device for search or assistance in translating or decrypting the information), can be acquired from another federal agency without individualized suspicion. Assistance for "subject matter expertise" from experts working in other federal agencies may be had only when there is reasonable suspicion of activities in violation of the laws enforced by CBP. The Directive states that reasonable suspicion may be based upon the presence of an individual on a government terrorist watch list.[86]

If probable cause arises after the border search of information, CBP officers are authorized to seize the electronic device being searched, or to make copies of the information from the device. If probable cause does not arise, "CBP may retain only information relating to immigration, customs, and other enforcement matters if such retention is consistent with the privacy and data protection standards of the system of records in which such information is retained."[87]

Immigration and Customs Enforcement Policy

Immigration and Customs Enforcement (ICE), the agency responsible for ensuring compliance with the federal immigration and customs laws, issued a directive on August 18, 2009, outlining the agency's policy and procedures regarding "the border search authority to search, detain, seize, retain, and share information contained in electronic devices possessed by individuals at the border, the functional equivalent of the border, and the extended border to ensure compliance with customs, immigration, and other laws enforced by ICE."[88]

The Directive asserts that "ICE Special Agents acting under border search authority may search, detain, seize, retain, and share electronic devices, or information contained therein, with or without individualized suspicion ..."[89]

The Directive states that consent is not needed to conduct a border search.[90] However, ICE Special Agents should conduct border searches "in the presence of, or with the knowledge of, the traveler" to the extent practicable.[91] When not practicable, because of "law enforcement, national security, or other operational concerns," ICE Special Agents must note the circumstances in appropriate ICE systems.[92] In addition, permitting an individual to be in the room where the search is conducted does not mean the individual will be allowed to witness the search. If allowing the individual to witness the search could reveal "law enforcement techniques or potentially compromise other operational concerns," the individual will not be permitted to witness the search.[93]

The Directive states that "Special Agents are to complete the search of detained electronic devices, or copies of information therefrom, in a reasonable time given the facts and circumstances of the particular search" with the circumstances noted.[94] Searches are "generally" to be finished within 30 days of the date of detention, unless circumstances warrant extra time. Any detention exceeding the 30 calendar days must be approved by a Group Supervisor or equivalent, and approved every 15 calendar days thereafter, with the specific justification for additional time noted.[95]

The Directive outlines the procedures ICE Special Agents must use when seeking assistance from other federal agencies or non-federal entities. According to the procedure, Special Agents are "responsible for ensuring that the results of the assistance are received in a reasonable time."[96] Special assistance may be required when a Special Agent, during the course of a border search, encounters information in an electronic device that "presents technical difficulties, is in a foreign language, and/or is encrypted."[97] Special Agents may demand "translation, decryption, and/or technical assistance" from other federal agencies or non-federal entities.[98] This demand may be made without individualized suspicion.[99] Special Agents may also encounter information that requires subject matter experts to determine whether the information is relevant to the laws enforced by ICE.[100] This demand can be made when a Special Agent has reasonable suspicion that a law enforced by ICE is being violated.[101] Special Agents may create and transmit copies of information to other federal agencies or non-federal entities for subject matter assistance.

However, the original electronic devices should only be transmitted when necessary for the subject matter assistance.[102] When a Special Agent determines there is probable cause of unlawful activity after reviewing information searched during a border search, the Special Agent may seize and retain both the device and the information.[103] All retained information from electronic devices determined to be of no relevance to ICE will be destroyed within seven business days after the conclusion of the border search unless circumstances require more time.[104] All destructions must be accomplished no later than 21 calendar days after conclusion of the search.[105]

According to the Directive, "all electronic devices crossing U.S. borders are subject to border search," and a claim of privilege or personal information will not prevent the search. However, certain types of information are subject to special handling by ICE Special Agents.[106] Business or commercial information is to be treated as business confidential information.[107] Legal information and other information claimed to be protected by attorney-client or attorney work privilege can be searched if the Special Agent suspects that the content of the information constitutes evidence of a crime or some other matter that falls within the jurisdiction of ICE. In such a case, the Special

Agent must consult the ICE Office of the Chief Counsel or the appropriate U.S. Attorney's Office before beginning the search. Other sensitive information, such as medical records or journalist work-related information will be handled pursuant to federal law and ICE policy, and questions regarding such review, shall be directed to the ICE Office of the Chief Counsel.

CONCLUSION

It is arguable that there is a higher expectation of privacy surrounding the contents of laptops than other types of physical property, such as vehicle interiors. Even when a vehicle search involves an onerous and time-consuming inspection of a gasoline tank, some would argue that the expectation of privacy surrounding the vehicle and its contents does not appear to be as high as the expectation of privacy regarding the contents of a laptop, which often contains private thoughts or other forms of privileged information. On the other hand, laptop searches are not considered by the courts as intrusive as strip or body-cavity searches, where the expectation of privacy surrounding one's body is considered higher.[108] Although the Ninth Circuit in *Arnold* has analogized laptop searches to all other searches of personalty, other federal circuits may agree with Judge Kozinski in holding that the government owes greater deference to the privacy interest surrounding laptops.

In addition to privacy interests, courts have taken a range of other concerns into account when determining whether reasonable suspicion must justify a warrantless border search. For example, when courts have conducted border search analyses, they have frequently considered potential harms resulting from illegal materials smuggled into the United States through laptops and electronic storage devices. As stated in *Ramsey*, "The border search exception is grounded in the recognized right of the sovereign to control ... who and what may enter the country."[109] Laptops can present a challenge to the nation's ability to control what enters its borders because the vast and compact storage capacity of laptops can be used to smuggle illegal materials. In light of this, courts have held that routine searches of laptops at the border may be justified because of the strong government interest in preventing the dissemination of child pornography and other forms of "obscene" material that may be contained in laptops.[110] Another justification may be to facilitate searches of laptops owned by suspected terrorists, which may contain information related to a planned terrorist attack.[111]

On the other hand, if customs officials can conduct laptop border searches without the need for reasonable suspicion, there is the potential for customs officials to conduct targeted searches based on justifications prohibited by the Constitution. For example, if a customs official could conduct a search without cause, it may be more difficult to detect unlawful bases for the searches because the official would not need to explain why he conducted the search. Such concerns suggest that resolving the issues surrounding laptop border searches will involve striking a careful balance between national security and civil liberties.

The Ninth Circuit, by equating the privacy interest implicated in personal information with that surrounding normal personal effects, has adopted a categorical approach to the border search doctrine. The court has concluded that the search of all personal property does not require reasonable suspicion unless the search is conducted in a manner that is destructive or particularly offensive.[112] So far, the Ninth Circuit is the only circuit to have explicitly stated that such searches do not require reasonable suspicion. Whether other federal circuits adopt this approach or, in the same vein as Judge Kozinksi, give credence to the notion that a heightened expectation of privacy surrounds expressive materials, thus requiring reasonable suspicion before being searched, is an open question.

LEGISLATIVE PROPOSALS

A bill introduced in the 111th Congress, the Securing our Borders and our Data Act of 2009 (H.R. 239), would prohibit laptop searches based solely on border search authority.[113] The legislation would establish "fundamental rules" prohibiting a federal border officer from searching or seizing a "digital electronic device" or "electronic storage media" based solely on the power of the United States to search and seize the effects of individuals seeking entry into the country. Instead, the legislation would allow such searches only in cases where border officers have reasonable suspicion that a device contains criminal evidence. Devices could be seized only if constitutional authority other than border search authority provided a justification. The bill would direct the Secretary of Homeland Security to promulgate rules regarding: maximum time periods during which border officers can detain devices;

owners' rights to retrieve detained devices; and strategies for maintaining the integrity of all information detained and shared with other government agencies.[114]

The Border Security Search Accountability Act of 2009 (H.R. 1726) would mandate that the Commissioner of Customs and Border Protection promulgate a rule with respect to the scope of procedural and record-keeping requirements associated with border security searches of electronic devices.[115] The rule would require that commercial information be handled in a manner consistent with all laws and regulations governing such information, that electronic searches be conducted in front of a supervisor, that a determination of the number of days such information could be retained without probable cause be made, that the individual whose information was seized be notified if the information is entered into an electronic database, that an individual receive a receipt if his device is seized during a border search, that an individual subject to a border search of an electronic device receive notice as to how he can report any abuses or concerns related to the search, that the rights of individuals with regard to border searches be posted at all ports of entry, that a privacy impact assessment of the rule be made, and that a civil rights impact assessment of the rule be made.[116]

Author Contact Information

Yule Kim
Legislative Attorney
ykim@crs.loc.gov, 7-9138

End Notes

[1] U.S. Const. Amend. IV.

[2] The Supreme Court has interpreted *probable cause* to mean "a fair probability that contraband or evidence of a crime will be found in a particular place." Illinois v. Gates, 462 U.S. 213, 238 (1983). *See also* Ornelas v. United States, 517 U.S. 690, 696 (1996).

[3] Katz v. United States, 389 U.S. 347, 357 (1967) ("[S]earches conducted outside the judicial process without prior approval by judge or magistrate are *per se* unreasonable under the Fourth Amendment—subject only to a few specifically established and well delineated exceptions.").

[4] For a more expansive treatment of the border search exception to the Fourth Amendment, see CRS Report RL3 1826, *Protecting the U.S. Perimeter: Border Searches Under the Fourth Amendment*, by Yule Kim.

[5] *See* Act of July 31, 1789, ch. 5 §§23-24, 1 Stat. 29, 43 (authorizing customs officials "full power and authority" to enter and search "any ship or vessel, in which they shall have reason to suspect any goods, wares or merchandise subject to duty shall be concealed ..."); Carroll v. United States, 267 U.S. 132, 153-154 (1925) ("Travellers may be so stopped in crossing an international boundary because of national self-protection reasonably requiring one entering the country to identify himself as entitled to come in, and his belongings as effects which may be lawfully brought in."). *Accord* Almeida-Sanchez v. United States, 413 U.S. 266 (1973); United States v. 12 200-Ft. Reels of Super 8mm. Film, 413 U.S. 123 (1973); United States v. Thirty-Seven (37) Photographs, 402 U.S. 363 (1971); Boyd v. United States, 116 U.S. 616 (1886).

[6] 431 U.S. 606, 619 (1977).

[7] *Id.* at 622.

[8] "Reasonable cause to suspect" appears to be equivalent to "reasonable suspicion," which is simply a particularized and objective basis for suspecting the particular person of wrongdoing. *See* Terry v. Ohio, 392 U.S. 1, 21 (1978).

[9] 431 U.S. at 614.

[10] *Id.* at 619 ("This longstanding recognition that searches at our borders without probable cause and without a warrant are nonetheless 'reasonable' has a history as old as the Fourth Amendment itself.").

[11] *See* United States v. Berisha, 925 F.2d 791, 795 (5th Cir. 1991) (extending the border search exception to routine outbound searches); United States v. Stanley, 545 F.2d 661, 667 (9th Cir. 1976), *cert. denied*, 436 U.S. 917 (1978); United States v. Ezeiruaku, 936 F.2d 136, 143 (3d Cir. 1991); United States v. Duncan, 693 F.2d 971, 977 (9th Cir. 1982); United States v. Ajlouny, 629 F.2d 830, 834 (2d Cir. 1980).

[12] *See* Almeida-Sanchez v. United States, 413 U.S. 266, 272-273 (1973); United States v. Hill, 939 F.2d 934, 936 (1 1th Cir. 1991); United States v. Gaviria, 805 F.2d 1108, 1112 (2d Cir. 1986). In the context of international airports, the border search exception only applies to searches of persons and effects on international flights, whereas the administrative search exception, which applies to routine searches with purposes unrelated to law enforcement, is used to justify searches of persons and effects on domestic flights. *See* United States v. Davis, 482 F.2d 893, 908-912 (9th Cir. 1973).

[13] 473 U.S. 531, 541 (1985) ("We have not previously decided what level of suspicion would justify a seizure of an incoming traveler for purposes other than a routine border search.").

[14] *Id.* at 535.

[15] *Id.*

[16] *Id.* at 541 ("We hold that the detention of a traveler at the border, beyond the scope of a routine customs search and inspection, is justified at its inception if customs agents, considering all the facts surrounding the traveler and her trip, reasonably suspect that the traveler is smuggling contraband in her alimentary canal.").

[17] *See* United States v. Flores-Montano, 541 U.S. 149, 154 *citing Terry*, 392 U.S. at 21 ("And in justifying the particular intrusion the police officer must be able to point to specific and articulable facts which, taken together with rational inferences from those facts, reasonably warrant that intrusion.").

[18] *Montoya de Hernandez*, 473 U.S. at 538 ("Routine searches of the persons and effects of entrants are not subject to any requirement of reasonable suspicion, probable cause, or warrant, and first-class mail may be opened without a warrant on less than probable cause.").

[19] *See* United States v. Ezeiruaku, 936 F.2d 136 (3d Cir. 1991); *Berisha*, 925 F.2d 791. *See also* United States v. Chaplinksi, 579 F.2d 373 (5th Cir. 1978); United States v. Lincoln, 494 F.2d 833 (9th Cir. 1974); United States v. Chavarria, 493 F.2d 935 (5th Cir. 1974); United States v. King, 483 F.2d 353 (10th Cir. 1973).

[20] 541 U.S. 149, 154 (2004).

[21] *Id.* ("It is difficult to imagine how the search of a gas tank, which should be solely a repository for fuel, could be more of an invasion of privacy than the search of the automobile's passenger compartment.").

[22] *See id. citing Terry*, 392 U.S. at 21 ("And in justifying the particular intrusion the police officer must be able to point to specific and articulable facts which, taken together with rational inferences from those facts, reasonably warrant that intrusion.").

[23] *See id.* at 541 n. 4.

[24] *Id.* (requiring "reasonable suspicion" for the detention of a traveler at the border, beyond the scope of a routine customs search and inspection). *See also* Henderson v. United States, 390 F.2d 805 (9th Cir. 1967) (holding that strip searches may be conducted only upon a real suspicion); United States v. Adekunle, 980 F.2d 985 (5th Cir. 1992), on reh'g, 2 F.3d 559 (5th Cir. 1993) (requiring reasonable suspicion to justify a strip search); United States v. Asbury, 586 F.2d 973, 975-976 (2d Cir. 1978) (requiring reasonable suspicion for strip searches); Rivas v. United States, 368 F.2d 703 (9th Cir. 1966) (requiring a clear indication of the possession of narcotics to justify an alimentary canal search).

[25] *Flores-Montano*, 541 U.S. at 152.

[26] *See, e.g.*, United States v. Ickes, 393 F.3d 501, 505 (4th Cir. 2005); United States v. Romm, 455 F.3d 990, 997 (9th Cir. 2006); United States v. Irving, 452 F.3d 110, 123 (2d Cir. 2006) ("An airport is considered the functional equivalent of a border and thus a search there may fit within the border search exception."); United States v. Furukawa, No. 06-145, slip op. (D. Minn., November 16, 2006), 2006 U.S. Dist. LEXIS 83767; United States v. Hampe, No. 07-3- B-W, slip op. (D. Me., April 18, 2007), 2007 U.S. Dist. LEXIS 29218.

[27] *See, e.g.*, *Irving*, 452 F.3d at 124 ("Because these searches were supported by reasonable suspicion, we need not determine whether they were routine or non-routine."); *Furukawa*, slip op. at *1-2 ("[T]he court need not determine whether a border search of a laptop is 'routine' for purposes of the Fourth Amendment because, regardless, the magistrate judge correctly found the customs official had a reasonable suspicion in this case.").

[28] *Ickes*, 393 F.3d at 507 (noting that the computer search did not begin until the customs agents found marijuana paraphernalia and child pornography which raised a reasonable suspicion); *Hampe*, slip op. at *4-5 (holding that even though the laptop search did not implicate any of the serious concerns that would characterize a search as non-routine, the peculiar facts of the case gave rise to reasonable suspicion).

[29] 533 F.3d 1003, 1008 (2008) ("We are satisfied that reasonable suspicion is not needed for customs officials to search a laptop or other personal electronic storage device at the border.").

[30] 393 F.3d 501 (4th Cir. 2005).

[31] *Id.* at 502.

[32] *Id.* at 503.

[33] *Id.*

[34] *Id.*

[35] *Id.* at 505.

[36] *Id.* at 507.

[37] *Id.* at 506.

[38] 455 F.3d 990 (9th Cir. 2006).

[39] *Id.* at 994.

[40] *Id.*

[41] *Id.*

[42] *Id.*

[43] *Id.* at 997.

[44] *Id.* at 996.

[45] *Id.*

[46] *Id.*

[47] *Id.* at 997.

[48] *Id.* (declining to consider the issue because arguments not raised by a party in its opening briefs are deemed waived).
[49] 533 F.3d 1003 (9th Cir. 2008).
[50] *Id.* at 1005.
[51] *Id.*
[52] *Id.*
[53] *Id.*
[54] *Id.* at 1007.
[55] *Id.* at 1007-1008.
[56] *Id.* at 1009.
[57] *Id.*
[58] *Id.* at 1008.
[59] *Id.*
[60] *Id.* at 1010.
[61] 547 F.3d 993 (9th Cir. 2008).
[62] *Id.* at 996.
[63] *Id.* at 1003.
[64] *Id.* at 1004.
[65] *Id.* at 1014 (Kozinski, J., dissenting).
[66] *Id.* at 1017-1019 (Kozinski, J., dissenting).
[67] *Id.* at 1017 (Kozinksi, J., dissenting) *citing Entick v. Harrington*, 19 Howell's State Trials 1029, 95 Eng. Rep. 807 (1765).
[68] *Id.* (Kozinski, J., dissenting).
[69] *Id.* at 1016. (Kozinski, J., dissenting).
[70] *Id.* at 1014-1015 (Kozinski, J., dissenting).
[71] For more details on CBP and ICE, *see generally* CRS Report RS2 1899, *Border Security: Key Agencies and Their Missions*, by Chad C. Haddal.
[72] Presumably, an *individualized suspicion* standard is synonymous with or perhaps even weaker than a *reasonable suspicion* standard. This is because the Supreme Court has rebuked the use by lower federal courts of standards of suspicion other than *probable cause* or *reasonable suspicion. See Montoya de Hernandez*, 473 U.S. at 541.
[73] Border Search of Electronic Devices Containing Information, CBP Directive No. 3340-049, § 1 (August 20, 2009).
[74] *Id.* at § 2 (August 20, 2009).
[75] Border Search of Electronic Devices Containing Information, CBP Directive No. 3 340-049, § 5.1 (August 20, 2009).
[76] *Id.* at § 5.2.
[77] *Id.* at § 5.2.1.
[78] *Id.* at § 5.2.2.
[79] *Id.* at § 5.2.3.
[80] *Id.* at §§ 5.2.2, 5.2.3.
[81] *Id.* at § 5.3.1.
[82] *Id.*
[83] *Id.* at § 5.3.1.1.
[84] *Id.* at § 5.3.1.2.
[85] *Id.* at §5.3.2.
[86] *Id.*
[87] *Id.* at § 5.4.
[88] Border Searches of Electronic Devices, ICE Directive No. 7-6.1, § 1.1 (August 18, 2009).
[89] *Id.* at § 6.1.
[90] *Id.* at § 8.1(3).
[91] *Id.* at § 8.1(2).
[92] *Id.*

[93] *Id.*
[94] *Id.* at § 8.3(1).
[95] *Id.*
[96] *Id.* at § 8.3(2).
[97] *Id.* at § 8.4(1)(a).
[98] *Id.*
[99] *Id.*
[100] *Id.* at § 8.4(2)(a).
[101] *Id.* at § 8.4(2)(b).
[102] *Id.* at § 8.4(4).
[103] *Id.* at § 8.5(1)(a).
[104] *Id.* at § 8.5(1)(e).
[105] *Id.*
[106] *Id.* at § 8.6(1).
[107] *Id.* at § 8.6(2)(a).
[108] *Chase*, 503 F.2d 571 (strip searches require reasonable suspicion); *Montoya de Hernandez*, 473 U.S. 531 (alimentary canal search justified by reasonable suspicion).
[109] *Ramsey*, 431 U.S. at 611.
[110] *See, e.g.*, New York v. Ferber, 458 U.S. 747, 765 (1982) (holding that child pornography does not enjoy First Amendment protections because the government has a compelling state interest in preventing the sexual abuse of children and that the distribution of child pornography is intrinsically related to that state interest).
[111] *See Ickes*, 393 F.3d at 506.
[112] *Arnold*, 533 F.3d at 1007-1008.
[113] The Securing our Borders and our Data Act of 2009, H.R. 239, 111th Cong. (2009).
[114] This legislation is identical to a bill introduced during the 1 10th Congress. *See* Securing Our Borders and Our Data Act of 2008, H.R. 6702, 1 10th Cong. (2008). Another related bill introduced during the 1 10th Congress, H.R. 6588, would have prohibited laptop searches based on the United States' border search authority but permitted laptop searches conducted under any other federal authority. *See* Electronic Device Privacy Act of 2008, H.R. 6588, 1 10th Cong. (2008).
[115] Border Security Search Accountability Act of 2009, H.R. 1726, 111th Cong. (2009).
[116] This bill is similar to H.R. 6869, introduced in the 1 10th Congress, which would have directed the Department of Homeland Security to issue rules regarding the scope and procedural requirements associated with border security searches of electronic devices. *See* Border Security Search Accountability Act of 2008, H.R. 6869, 110th Cong. (2008).

In: The Fourth Amendment
Editors: Jesse V. Kessler
ISBN: 978-1-61728-885-2

Chapter 3

GOVERNMENT ACCESS TO PHONE CALLING ACTIVITY AND RELATED RECORDS: LEGAL AUTHORITIES

Elizabeth B. Bazan, Edward C. Liu and Gina Stevens

SUMMARY

Public interest in the means by which the government may collect telephone call records has been raised by ongoing revelations regarding alleged intelligence activity by the National Security Agency (NSA) and the Federal Bureau of Investigation (FBI). According to a *USA Today* article from May 11, 2006, the NSA allegedly sought and obtained records of telephone numbers called and received from millions of telephones within the United States from three telephone service providers; a fourth reportedly refused to provide such records. Additionally, a series of reports issued by the Department of Justice's Office of the Inspector General (DOJ OIG), most recently in January of 2010, indicate that, between 2002 and 2006, consumer records held by telephone companies had been provided to the FBI through the use of "exigent letters" and other informal methods that fell outside of the national security letter (NSL) process embodied in statute and internal FBI policies.

The Supreme Court has held that there is no Fourth Amendment protection of telephone calling records held in the hands of third party providers, where the content of any call is not intercepted. However, this report summarizes existing *statutory* authorities regarding access by the government, for either foreign intelligence or law enforcement purposes, to information related to telephone calling patterns or practices. Where pertinent, it also discusses statutory prohibitions against accessing or disclosing such information, along with relevant exceptions to those prohibitions.

Statutory provisions authorizing, pursuant to court order, the use of pen registers and trap and trace devices exist in both the Foreign Intelligence Surveillance Act (FISA), 50 U.S.C. § 1841 *et seq.*, and, for law enforcement purposes, in 18 U.S.C. § 3121 *et seq.*

FISA's "business records" provision, 50 U.S.C. § 1861, provides authority, pursuant to court order, for requests for production of "any tangible thing" relevant to collection of foreign intelligence information not concerning a U.S. person, or relevant to an investigation into international terrorism or clandestine intelligence activities. Under 50 U.S.C. § 1861, an investigation concerning a U.S. person may not be based solely on activities protected by the First Amendment.

Access to stored electronic communications is addressed in 18 U.S.C. § 2701 *et seq.* 18 U.S.C. § 2702 prohibits voluntary disclosure of customer communications records by a service provider unless it falls within one of several exceptions. Required disclosure of customer records to the government under certain circumstances is addressed under 18 U.S.C. § 2703, including, among others, disclosure pursuant to a warrant or grand jury or trial subpoena. 18 U.S.C. § 2709 is a national security letter provision, under which a wire or electronic service provider may be compelled to provide subscriber information and toll billing records information, or electronic communication transactional records in its custody or possession.

Finally, § 222 of the Communications Act of 1934, as amended, protects customer proprietary network information, and violations of pertinent provisions of law or regulation may expose service providers to criminal sanctions, civil penalties, and forfeiture provisions.

Public interest in the means by which the government may collect telephone call records has been raised by ongoing revelations regarding alleged intelligence activity by the National Security Agency (NSA) and the Federal Bureau of Investigation (FBI). According to a *USA Today* article from May 11, 2006, the NSA allegedly sought and obtained records of telephone numbers called and received from millions of telephones within the United States from three telephone service providers; a fourth reportedly refused to provide such records.[1] Additionally, a series of reports issued by the

Department of Justice's Office of the Inspector General (DOJ OIG), most recently in January of 2010, indicate that, between 2002 and 2006, consumer records held by telephone companies had been provided to the FBI through the use of "exigent letters" and other informal methods that fell outside of the national security letter (NSL) process embodied in statute and internal FBI policies.[2] These reports also indicate that records may have been sought without demonstrating a relationship to an active investigation.[3]

This report summarizes legal authorities regarding access by the government, for either foreign intelligence or law enforcement purposes, to information related to telephone calling patterns or practices. Where pertinent, it also discusses statutory prohibitions against accessing or disclosing such information, along with relevant exceptions to those prohibitions.

TELEPHONE RECORDS AND THE FOURTH AMENDMENT

The Supreme Court, in *Smith v. Maryland*, 442 U.S. 735 (1979), in a pen register case,[4] has held that there is no Fourth Amendment protected reasonable expectation of privacy in records of telephone calls held in the hands of third party providers, where the content of any call is not intercepted. The Fourth Amendment to the United States Constitution guarantees:

> The right of the people to be secure in their persons, houses, papers, and effects, against unreasonable searches and seizures, shall not be violated, and no Warrants shall issue, but upon probable cause, supported by Oath or affirmation, and particularly describing the place to be searched, and the persons or things to be seized.[5]

Whether the use of a pen register is a "search and seizure" within the meaning of the Fourth Amendment determines if the government, in compliance with the Constitution, must secure a warrant or court order prior to its installation. In 1979, the United States Supreme Court decided this question in *Smith v. Maryland,*[6] holding that the Fourth Amendment does not prohibit the use of pen registers without a warrant. Writing the majority opinion joined by four other justices, Justice Harry Blackmun drew a distinction between the acquisition of contents of telephone communications using electronic listening devices, which the Court in *Katz v. United States*[7] had deemed to be a "search" under the Fourth Amendment, and the capture of electronic impulses that identify the numbers dialed on a telephone using a pen register device.

According to the majority in *Smith,* it is a constitutionally significant difference that pen registers do not record the *contents* of communications, in contrast to the listening devices employed in *Katz.*[8] The Court explained that the Fourth Amendment does not apply to the use of pen registers because individuals do not have a legitimate expectation of privacy against invasion by government action, that protects the numbers dialed into a telephone system:

> All telephone users realize that they must "convey" phone numbers to the telephone company, since it is through telephone company switching equipment that their calls are completed. All subscribers realize, moreover, that the phone company has facilities for making permanent records of the numbers they dial, for they see a list of their long-distance (toll) calls on their monthly bills. In fact, pen registers and similar devices are routinely used by telephone companies "for the purposes of checking billing operations, detecting fraud, and preventing violations of law."[9]

The Court stated that telephone customers, by voluntarily conveying phone numbers to the telephone company and "expos[ing] that information to its equipment in the ordinary course of business," assume the risk that the company may disclose such information to law enforcement.[10] Because there is no actual or legitimate expectation of privacy in the numbers dialed from a telephone, the installation and use of a pen register is not a "search" requiring a warrant under the Fourth Amendment, the Court ruled.[11]

In contrast, the dissenting opinions in *Smith* concluded that telephone numbers dialed from a phone are entitled to the same constitutional protection that telephone conversations receive under *Katz* because such numbers are not without "content" - they "reveal the identities of the persons and the places called, and thus reveal the most intimate details of a person's life."[12] Furthermore, the dissenters objected to the majority's characterization that the use of a telephone involves an assumption of risk on the part of the customer that telephone dialing information might be disclosed to the government; assumption of risk generally requires there to have been a choice to engage in the activity, and "as a practical matter, individuals have no realistic alternative" to the use of a telephone. [13]

Although the protections of the Fourth Amendment may not reach records of telephone calls held by third parties, Congress has enacted a number of statutes since the *Smith* decision that both permit access by the government for foreign intelligence or law enforcement purposes to information relating to telephone numbers dialed from or received by a particular telephone number, as well as duration and usage, while simultaneously imposing limitations as to how such information may be accessed and under what circumstances it may be used.

STATUTORY PROVISIONS

Information regarding telephone calling patterns, duration, usage, and length of service may be sought by the government directly through the use of pen registers[14] or trap and trace devices. [15] Statutory provisions authorizing, pursuant to court order, the use of pen registers and trap and trace devices exist in both the Foreign Intelligence Surveillance Act (FISA), 50 U.S.C. § 1841 *et seq*., and, for law enforcement purposes, in 18 U.S.C. § 3121 *et seq*.

Telephone calling activity may also be collected indirectly by seeking telephone toll or transactional records from third party providers. For example, FISA's "business records" provision, 50 U.S.C. § 1861, authorizes court orders to compel the production of "any tangible thing" relevant to collection of foreign intelligence information not concerning a U.S. person, or relevant to an investigation into international terrorism or clandestine intelligence activities.[16]

Access to stored electronic communications is also addressed in 18 U.S.C. § 2701 *et seq.* 18 U.S.C. § 2702 prohibits voluntary disclosure of customer communications records by a service provider unless it falls within one of several exceptions. Required disclosure of customer records to the government under certain circumstances is addressed under 18 U.S.C. § 2703, including, among others, disclosure pursuant to a warrant or grand jury or trial subpoena. 18 U.S.C. § 2709 is a national security letter provision,[17] under which a wire or electronic service provider[18] may be compelled to provide subscriber information and toll billing records information, or electronic communication transactional records in its custody or possession in response to a request by the Director of the Federal Bureau of Investigation (FBI) if the Director of the FBI, or his designee in a position not lower than Deputy Assistant Director at Bureau headquarters or a Special Agent in Charge designated by the FBI Director in a field office, certifies that the records or information sought is relevant to an authorized investigation to protect against international terrorism or clandestine intelligence activities, provided that such an investigation of a U.S. person is not conducted solely on the basis of First Amendment protected activities.

Finally, § 222 of the Communications Act of 1934, as amended, 47 U.S.C. § 222, restricts the voluntary disclosure of customer proprietary network information by telecommunications service providers. Violations of the pertinent provisions of law or regulation may expose service providers to criminal sanctions, civil penalties and forfeiture provisions, 47 U.S.C. §§ 501-503.[19]

Each of these statutory schemes is described in more detail below.

Pen Registers and Trap and Trace Devices for Foreign Intelligence and International Terrorism Investigations under FISA

Under 50 U.S.C. § 1842,[20] the Attorney General or a designated attorney for the government may apply for an ex parte court order authorizing the use of a pen register or trap and trace device to a Foreign Intelligence Surveillance Court (FISC) judge or to a U.S. magistrate judge designated by the Chief Justice of the United States to have the power to hear applications or grant orders approving installation and use of a pen register or trap and trace device on behalf of an FISC judge. The application must be approved by the Attorney General or a designated government attorney; must identify the federal officer seeking to use the pen register or trap and trace device; and must include a certification that the information likely to be obtained is foreign intelligence information[21] not concerning a U.S. person[22] or that the information is relevant to an ongoing investigation to protect against international terrorism or clandestine intelligence activities. An investigation of a U.S. person may not be conducted solely on the basis of First Amendment protected activities.

The order must specify the identity of the person who is the subject of the investigation, if known. If known, the order must identify the person to whom the telephone line or other facility to which the pen register or trap and trace device is to be attached is leased or in whose name it is listed. In addition, the order must list the attributes of the communications to which it applies, such as the number or other identifier and, if known, the location of the telephone line or other facility involved. In the case of a trap and trace device, the order must also identify the geographic limits of the trap and trace order.

Such an order, at the request of the applicant, also directs the provider of the wire or electronic service, landlord, custodian, or other person, to furnish any information, facilities, or technical assistance needed to accomplish the installation and operation of the pen register or trap and trace device in a manner that will protect its secrecy and minimize interference with the services provided. In addition, the order directs the provider, landlord, custodian, or other person not to disclose the existence of the investigation or the pen register or trap and trace device to anyone unless or until ordered to do so by the court. Records concerning the pen register or trap and trace device or the aid furnished are to be kept under security procedures approved by the Attorney General and the Director of National Security under 50 U.S.C. § 1 805(b)(2)(C). The order also directs the applicant for the order to provide compensation for reasonable expenses incurred by the provider, landlord, custodian, or other person in providing information, facilities, or technical assistance.

Under 50 U.S.C. § 1842(d)(2)(C)(i), upon the request of the applicant for the court order, the court shall direct the wire or electronic service provider to provide the federal officer using the pen register or trap and trace device with the name; address; and the telephone number, instrument number or subscriber number or identifier of the customer or subscriber using the service covered by the order for the period specified by the order, including temporarily assigned network address or associated routing or transmission information. The service provider must also provide, if so ordered by the court upon the applicant's request, information on length of service of the customer or subscriber, as well as local or long distance telephone records of the subscriber or customer, and, if applicable, any records on periods of usage by the customer or subscriber. Further, the court, at the applicant's request, may order disclosure by the service provider of any mechanisms and sources of payment for the service (i.e., credit card, bank account).

Similarly, under 50 U.S.C. § 1842(d)(2)(C)(ii), if the information is available with respect to any customer or subscriber of incoming or outgoing communications to or from the service covered by the order, the court, upon the request of the applicant for the order, is to direct the wire or electronic service provider to provide the name; address; telephone number, instrument number or other subscriber number or identifier, of such customer or subscriber, as well as length of service provided to and types of serviced utilized by the subscriber or customer.

In general, the duration of an order issued under this section is not to exceed 90 days, with the possibility of extension for periods of not more than 90 days. However, if the applicant for the order certifies that the information likely to be obtained is foreign intelligence information not concerning a United States person, then an extension may be for up to a year. No cause of action may be brought against any wire or electronic service provider, landlord, custodian, or other person that furnishes information, facilities, or technical assistance pursuant to an order issued under this provision. Unless otherwise ordered by the judge, the results of the pen register or trap and trace device are to be provided to the authorized government official or officials at reasonable intervals.

Under 50 U.S.C. § 1805(i), as added by the FISA Amendments Act of 2008,[23] if an FISC judge grants an application by the government to conduct electronic surveillance under FISA, then, upon the request of the applicant, the FISC judge shall also authorize the installation and use of pen registers and trap and trace devices. In such circumstances, the provisions of 50 U.S.C. § 1 842(d)(2) regarding disclosure of customer or subscriber information to the government would apply.

Pen Registers or Trap and Trace Devices Generally, and for Use in an Ongoing Criminal Investigation

18 U.S.C. § 3121 prohibits the installation and use of a pen register or trap and trace device without first obtaining a court order under FISA or under 18 U.S.C. § 3123. This prohibition does not apply to use by an electronic or wire service provider relating to:

- the operation, maintenance and testing of a service or protection of the rights or property of the service provider;
- the protection of users of the service from abuse or unlawful use of the service;
- to recording of the fact that a wire or electronic communication was initiated or completed to protect the service provider, another provider furnishing service toward completion of the wire communication, or a user of the service from fraudulent, unlawful or abusive use of the service; or
- to use where the consent of the user of the service has been obtained.

A government agency authorized to install and use a pen register or trap and trace device under the provisions of this chapter of Title 18, U.S.C., or under state law must use technology reasonably available to it that restricts the recording or decoding of electronic or other impulses to the dialing, routing, addressing, and signaling information utilized in the processing and transmitting of wire or electronic communications in a manner that does not include the contents of that communication.

An application for a court order authorizing a pen register or trap and trace device under this chapter must be made pursuant to 18 U.S.C. § 3122 in writing under oath or affirmation to a court of competent jurisdiction. Such an application must include the identity of the attorney for the government or the state law enforcement or investigative officer making the application and the identity of the law enforcement agency conducting the investigation, as well as a certification by the applicant that the information likely to be obtained is relevant to an ongoing criminal investigation being conducted by that agency.

Under 18 U.S.C. § 3123, the court shall enter an ex parte order authorization installation and use of a pen register or trap and trace device anywhere in the United States if the court finds that the applicant for the order has made such a certification. An order may authorize installation and use of a pen register or trap and trace device for a period of up to 60 days, which can be extended by court order for additional periods of no more than 60 days. The order must also direct that the order be sealed until otherwise ordered by the court, and must prohibit the person owning or leasing the line or other facility to which the pen register or trap and trace device is attached or applied, or who is obligated by the order to assist the applicant, from disclosing the existence of the pen register or trap and trace device or of the investigation to the listed subscriber or to any other person unless or until the court orders otherwise.[24]

Access to Business Records for Foreign Intelligence and International Terrorism Investigations

Under 50 U.S.C. § 1861, the Director of the Federal Bureau of Investigation (FBI) or a designee of the Director, whose rank shall not be lower than Assistant Special Agent in Charge, may apply to the FISA court for an order granting the government access to any tangible item (including books, records, papers, documents, and other items) for an investigation to obtain foreign intelligence information not concerning a United States person, or to protect against international terrorism or clandestine intelligence activities. Such an investigation of a United States person may not be conducted solely upon the basis of activities protected by the first amendment to the Constitution.

The application for such an order must include a statement of facts demonstrating that there are reasonable grounds to believe that the tangible things sought are relevant to an authorized or preliminary investigation to protect against international terrorism or espionage, or to obtain foreign intelligence information not concerning a U.S. person.[25] However, certain tangible items are deemed presumptively relevant to an investigation if the application's statement of facts shows that the items sought pertain to a foreign power or an agent of a foreign power, the activities of a suspected agent of a foreign power who is the subject of such authorized investigation, or an individual in contact with, or known to, a suspected agent of a foreign power who is the subject of such authorized investigation.[26]

The FISA court judge shall approve an application for an order under 50 U.S.C. § 1861, as requested or as modified, upon a finding that the application complies with statutory requirements. The order must contain a particularized description of the items sought, provide for a reasonable time to assemble them, and be limited to things which may be obtained under a grand jury subpoena or an order of a U.S. court for production of records or tangible things.[27] The order to produce the tangible things (production order) is also accompanied by a nondisclosure requirement (nondisclosure order) that prohibits the recipient from disclosing to any other person that the FBI has sought the tangible things described in the order, with limited exceptions.[28]

The recipient may immediately challenge the legality of the production order by filing a petition with the FISA court; however, the recipient must wait one year before challenging the nondisclosure order.[29] A FISA court judge considering the recipient's petition to modify or set aside the production order may do so only if the judge finds that the order does not meet statutory requirements or is otherwise unlawful.[30] A nondisclosure order may be modified or set aside if the judge finds that there is no reason to believe that disclosure may endanger the national security of the United States; interfere with a criminal, counterterrorism, or counterintelligence investigation; interfere with diplomatic relations; or endanger the life or physical safety of any person.[31] If, at the time the individual files the petition for judicial review of a nondisclosure order, the Attorney General, Deputy Attorney General, an Assistant Attorney General, or the Director of the FBI certifies that disclosure may endanger the national security of the United States or interfere with diplomatic relations, then the FISA judge must treat such government certification as conclusive unless the judge finds that the certification was made in bad faith.[32]

Authority to collect communications records under FISA is currently set to expire on December 31, 2009. After this date, and absent congressional extension, only records from common carriers, public accommodation facilities, storage facilities, and vehicle rental facilities may be sought under FISA.[33]

Access to Stored Electronic Communications and Transactional Records

Access to stored electronic communications and transactional records is addressed in 18 U.S.C. § 2701 *et seq.* Under 18 U.S.C. § 2702, voluntary disclosure of customer communications records by a service provider is prohibited unless it falls within one of several exceptions, including

- disclosure as authorized in 18 U.S.C. § 2703;
- disclosure with the lawful consent of the customer or subscriber; or
- disclosure to a governmental entity, if the provider, in good faith, believes that an emergency involving danger of death or serious physical injury to any person requires disclosure without delay of information relating to the emergency.[34]

In various reports regarding the use of "exigent letters," the DOJ OIG noted that one of the justifications for the use of exigent letters and other informal governmental requests for telephone records had been based upon this voluntary emergency disclosure provision.[35] However, these reports also concluded that many of the situations in which these tools were used did not appear to meet the emergency standard provided by this exception.[36]

Under 18 U.S.C. § 2703, a provider of electronic communication service or remote computing service shall disclose to a government entity the name, address, local and long distance telephone connection records, or records of session times and durations, length of service and types of service utilized, telephone instrument number or other subscriber number or identity, including temporarily assigned network address, and means and source of payment for such service pursuant to

- a warrant;
- a court order based upon specific and articulable facts showing that there are reasonable grounds to believe that the contents of a wire or electronic communication or the records or other information sought are relevant and material to an ongoing criminal investigation;

- customer or subscriber consent;
- a written request from the governmental entity relevant to a law enforcement investigation regarding telemarketing fraud;
- an administrative subpoena authorized by federal or state statute, or
- a federal or state grand jury subpoena or trial subpoena.

A governmental entity receiving such records or information is not required to provide notice to a subscriber or customer. Nor does any cause of action lie against any service provider of wire or electronic communication service, its officers, employees, agents, or other specified persons for providing information, facilities, or assistance in accordance with the terms of a court order, warrant, subpoena, statutory authorization or certification under this chapter.

18 U.S.C. § 2706 requires a government entity obtaining records or other information under §§ 2702 or 2703 to reimburse the costs reasonably necessary and directly incurred in searching for, assembling, reproducing or otherwise providing such information. The amount of payment is to be mutually agreed upon by the government entity and the person or entity providing the information, or, in the absence of an agreement, determined by the court issuing the production order. The reimbursement requirement does not apply to records or other information maintained by a communications common carrier that relate to telephone records and telephone listings obtained under 18 U.S.C. § 2703 unless a court orders payment upon a determination that the information required is unusually voluminous in nature or otherwise caused an undue burden upon the provider.

National Security Letters

Under 18 U.S.C. § 2709, a national security letter provision,[37] wire or electronic service providers[38] must provide subscriber information and toll billing records information, or electronic communication transactional records in its custody or possession in response to a request by the Director of the Federal Bureau of Investigation (FBI) if the Director of the FBI, or his designee in a position not lower than Deputy Assistant Director at Bureau headquarters or a Special Agent in Charge designated by the FBI Director in a field office, certifies that the records or information sought is relevant to an authorized investigation to protect against international terrorism or clandestine intelligence activities, provided that such an investigation of a U.S. person is not conducted solely on the basis of First Amendment protected activities.

Under 18 U.S.C. § 2709(b), if the Director of the Federal Bureau of Investigation, or his designee, certifies that disclosure of the request may result in a danger to the national security of the United States, interference with a criminal, counterterrorism, or counterintelligence investigation, interference with diplomatic relations, or danger to the life or physical safety of any person, no wire or electronic communications service provider, or officer, employee, or agent thereof, shall disclose to any person (other than those to whom such disclosure is necessary to comply with the request or an attorney to obtain legal advice or legal assistance with respect to the request) that the Federal Bureau of Investigation has sought or obtained access to information or records under this section.[39] The FBI must notify the person or entity to whom a §2709(b) request is made where such a nondisclosure requirement is applicable. A recipient of such a request who notifies those to whom notice is necessary for compliance with the request or who notifies an attorney to obtain legal advice or legal assistance with respect to the request must also advise them of the nondisclosure requirement.

At the request of the Director of the Federal Bureau of Investigation or the designee of the Director, any person making or intending to make a disclosure under this section shall identify to the Director or such designee the person to whom such disclosure will be made or to whom such disclosure was made prior to the request, except that nothing in this section shall require a person to inform the Director or such designee of the identity of an attorney to whom disclosure was made or will be made to obtain legal advice or legal assistance with respect to the request.

The FBI may only disseminate records obtained under this section as provided in guidelines approved by the Attorney General for foreign intelligence collection and foreign counterintelligence investigations conducted by the Federal Bureau of Investigation, and, with respect to dissemination to an agency of the United States, only if such information is clearly relevant to the authorized responsibilities of such agency. On a semiannual basis, the Director of the Federal Bureau of Investigation is required to fully inform the Permanent Select Committee on Intelligence of the House of Representatives and the Select Committee on Intelligence of the Senate, and the Committee on the Judiciary of the House of Representatives and the Committee on the Judiciary of the Senate, concerning all requests made under subsection (b) of this section.

Penalties

Except as provided in 18 U.S.C. § 2703(e), 18 U.S.C. § 2707 provides a civil cause of action for any provider of electronic communication service, subscriber, or other person aggrieved by a knowing or intentional violation of this chapter. The aggrieved party may receive equitable relief and damages. The damages which may be assessed by the court are actual damages suffered by the plaintiff plus any profits made by the violator as a result of the violation. At a minimum, a person entitled to recover damages must receive no less than $1,000. If a court or appropriate department or agency determines that the United States has violated this chapter and that the circumstances surrounding the violation raise questions as to whether a federal officer or employee acted willfully or intentionally with respect to the violation, disciplinary action against that officer or employee may also be initiated.

A person aggrieved by a willful violation of this chapter or a willful violation of 50 U.S.C. § 1845(a), which deals with the use of information gathered through a pen register and trap and trace under FISA, may commence a civil action against the United States in a U.S. district court to receive money damages under 18 U.S.C. § 2712. If the claim is successful in establishing such a violation, the court may assess actual damages, but not less than $10,000, whichever is greater, plus reasonably incurred litigation costs. There is a two year statute of limitations applicable to this provision, and this section states that this is the exclusive remedy against the United States for claims within the purview of the section. The agency or department must reimburse any award under this section to the U.S. treasury. Administrative discipline may also be pursued. A proceeding under 18 U.S.C. § 2712 shall be stayed by the court, upon motion by the United States, if the court determines that civil discovery will adversely affect the government's ability to conduct a related investigation or prosecution of a related criminal case. Such a stay also tolls the statute of limitations.

Communications Act of 1934

Telecommunications carriers are also subject to obligations to guard the confidentiality of customer proprietary network information (CPNI) and to ensure that it is not disclosed to third parties without customer approval or as required by law. Section 222 of the Communication Act of 1934, as amended, establishes a duty of every telecommunications carrier to protect the confidentiality of its customers' customer proprietary network information.[40]

Section 222 attempts to achieve a balance between marketing and customer privacy.

CPNI includes personally identifiable information derived from a customer's relationship with a telephone company, irrespective of whether the customer purchases landline or wireless telephone service. CPNI is defined as

> (A) information that relates to the quantity, technical configuration, type, destination, location, and amount of use of a telecommunications service subscribed to by any customer of a telecommunications carrier, and that is made available to the carrier by the customer solely by virtue of the carrier-customer relationship; and (B) information contained in the bills pertaining to telephone exchange service or telephone toll service received by a customer of a carrier.[41]

CPNI includes customers' calling activities and history (e.g., phone numbers called, frequency, duration, and time), and billing records.[42] It does not include subscriber list information, such as name, address, and phone number.[43]

In section 222, Congress created a framework to govern telecommunications carriers' use of information obtained through provision of a telecommunications service. Section 222 of the act provides that telecommunications carriers must protect the confidentiality of customer proprietary network information. The act limits carriers' abilities to use customer phone records, including for their own marketing purposes, without customer approval and appropriate safeguards. The act also prohibits carriers from using, disclosing, or permitting access to this information without the approval of the customer, or as otherwise required by law, if the use or disclosure is not in connection with the provided service.

Section 222(a) imposes a general duty on telecommunications carriers to protect the confidentiality of proprietary information of other carriers, equipment manufacturers, and customers.[44] Section 222(b) states that a carrier that receives or obtains proprietary information from other carriers in order to provide a telecommunications service may use such information only for that purpose and may not use that information for its own marketing efforts.[45]

The confidentiality protections applicable to customer proprietary network information are established in section 222(c). Subsection (c)(1) constitutes the core privacy requirement for telecommunications carriers.

> Except as required by law or with the approval of the customer, a telecommunications carrier that receives or obtains customer proprietary

> network information by virtue of its provision of a telecommunications service shall only use, disclose, or permit access to individually identifiable customer proprietary network information in its provision of (A) the telecommunications service from which such information is derived, or (B) services necessary to, or used in, the provision of such telecommunications service, including the publishing of directories.[46]

Section 222(c)(2) provides that a carrier must disclose CPNI "upon affirmative written request by the customer, to any person designated by the customer."[47] Section 222(c)(3) provides that a carrier may use, disclose, or permit access to aggregate customer information other than for the purposes described in subsection (1).[48] Thus, the general principle of confidentiality for customer information is that a carrier may only use, disclose, or permit access to customers' individually identifiable CPNI in limited circumstances: (1) as required by law;[49] (2) with the customer's approval; or (3) in its provision of the telecommunications service from which such information is derived, or services necessary to or used in the provision of such telecommunications service.

Exceptions to the general principle of confidentiality permit carriers to use, disclose, or permit access to customer proprietary network information to (1) initiate, render, bill, and collect for telecommunications services; (2) protect the rights or property of the carrier, the customers, and other carriers from fraudulent, abusive, or unlawful use of, or subscription to, such services; (3) provide any inbound telemarketing, referral, or administrative services to the customer for the duration of the call; and (4) provide call location information concerning the user of a commercial mobile service for emergency.[50]

Section 222(e) addresses the disclosure of subscriber list information, and permits carriers to provide subscriber list information to any person upon request for the purpose of publishing directories. The term "subscriber list information" means any information identifying the listed names of subscribers of a carrier and such subscribers' telephone numbers, addresses, or primary advertising classifications, or any combination of such listed names, numbers, addresses, or classifications; that the carrier or an affiliate has published, caused to be published, or accepted for publication in any directory format.[51]

Customer Proprietary Network Information (CPNI) Regulations

In 1998, the Federal Communications Commission issued its *CPNI Order* to implement section 222.[52] The *CPNI Order* and subsequent orders issued by the Commission govern the use and disclosure of customer proprietary network information by telecommunications carriers. When the FCC implemented Section 222, telecommunications carriers were required to obtain express consent from their customers (i.e., "opt-in consent") before a carrier could use customer phone records to market services outside of the customer's relationship with the carrier. The United States Court of Appeals for the Tenth Circuit struck down those rules, finding that they violated the First and Fifth Amendments of the Constitution.[53]

Subsequently, the FCC amended its CPNI regulations to require telecommunications carriers to receive opt-in (affirmative) consent before disclosing CPNI to third parties or affiliates that do not provide communications-related services.[54] However, carriers are permitted to disclose CPNI to affiliated parties after obtaining a customer's "opt-out" consent.[55] "Opt-Out" consent means that the telephone company sends the customer a notice saying it will consider the customer to have given approval to use the customer's information for marketing unless the customer tells it not to do so (usually within 30 days.)[56] Carriers are required, prior to soliciting the customer's approval, to provide notice to the customer of the customer's right to restrict use, disclosure, and access to the customer's CPNI.[57] Carriers are also required to establish safeguards to protect against the unauthorized disclosure of CPNI, including requirements that carriers maintain records that track access to customer CPNI records.[58] Each carrier is also required to certify annually its compliance with the CPNI requirements and to make this certification publicly available.[59] The FCC recently proposed $100,000 fines on telephone companies with inadequate certifications regarding compliance with FCC rules protecting customer information from disclosure.[60] A suit challenging the opt-in requirement is currently pending before the D.C. Circuit.[61]

Penalties

Carriers in violation of the CPNI requirements are subject to a variety of penalties under the act. Under the criminal penalty provision in section 501 of the act, 47 U.S.C. § 501, any person who willfully and knowingly does, causes or allows to be done, any act, matter, or thing prohibited by the act or declared unlawful, or who willfully and knowingly omits or fails to do what is required by the act, or who willfully or knowingly causes or allows such omission or failure, shall be punished for any such offense for which no penalty (other than a forfeiture) is provided by the act by a fine up to $10,000, imprisonment up to one year, or both, and in the case of a person previously convicted of violating the act, a fine up to $10,000, imprisonment up to two years, or both.

Section 502 of the act, 47 U.S.C. § 502, punishes willful and knowing violations of Federal Communication Commission regulations. Any person who willfully and knowingly violates any rule, regulation, restriction, or condition made or imposed by the Commission is, in addition to other penalties provided by law, subject to a maximum fine of $500 for each day on which a violation occurs.[62]

Under section 503(b)(1) of the act, 47 U.S.C. § 503(b)(1), any person who is determined by the Commission to have willfully or repeatedly failed to comply with any provision of the act or any rule, regulation, or order issued by the Commission shall be liable to the United States for a civil money "forfeiture" penalty.[63] Section 312(f)(1) of the act, 47 U.S.C. § 312(f)(1), defines "willful" as "the conscious and deliberate commission or omission of [any] act, irrespective of any intent to violate" the law. "Repeated" means that the act was committed or omitted more than once, or lasts more than one day. If the violator is a common carrier, section 503(b) authorizes the Commission to assess a forfeiture penalty of up to $130,000 for each violation or for each day of a continuing violation, except that the amount assessed for any continuing violation shall not exceed a total of $1,325,000 for any single act or failure to act.[64] To impose such a forfeiture penalty, the Commission must issue a notice of apparent liability, and the person against whom the notice has been issued must have an opportunity to show, in writing, why no such forfeiture penalty should be imposed. The Commission will then issue a forfeiture if it finds by a preponderance of the evidence that the person has violated the act or a Commission rule.

Author Contact Information

Elizabeth B. Bazan
Legislative Attorney
ebazan@crs.loc.gov, 7-7202

Gina Stevens
Legislative Attorney
gstevens@crs.loc.gov, 7-2581

Edward C. Liu
Legislative Attorney
eliu@crs.loc.gov, 7-9166

End Notes

[1] Leslie Cauley, *NSA Has Massive Database of Americans' Phone Calls; 3 Telecoms Help Government Collect Billions of Domestic Records*, USA TODAY, May 11, 2006, at 1A. The story alleged that Verizon, BellSouth, and AT&T provided calling records in response to the NSA's inquiry or production demand, while Qwest did not. In December of 2008, more revelations regarding an alleged NSA program, given the codename "Stellar Wind," were reported in the December 22, 2008, issue of *Newsweek*. *See* Michael Isikoff, *The Fed Who Blew the Whistle*, NEWSWEEK, Dec. 22, 2008, at 40, 44.

[2] U.S. DEPARTMENT OF JUSTICE, OFFICE OF THE INSPECTOR GENERAL, *A Review of the Federal Bureau of Investigation's Use of Exigent Letters and Other Informal Requests for Telephone Records* (Jan. 2010), available at *http://www.justice.gov/oig/special/s1001r.pdf;* U.S. DEPARTMENT OF JUSTICE, OFFICE OF THE INSPECTOR GENERAL, *A Review of the Federal Bureau of Investigation's Use of National Security Letters*, at 96 (March 2007), available at http://www.usdoj.gov/oig/special/s0703b/final.pdf.

[3] *Id.* at 92-93.

[4] A pen register is a device or process which records the dialing, routing, addressing, or signaling information transmitted in conjunction with an electronic communication, but does not record the contents of that communication. *See* 18 U.S.C. § 3127(3).

[5] U.S. CONST. amend. IV.

[6] 442 U.S. 735 (1979).

[7] 389 U.S. 347 (1967).

[8] *Smith*, 442 U.S. at 741 (emphasis in original).

[9] *Id.* at 742 (quoting United States v. New York Tel. Co., 434 U.S. 159, 174-75 (1977)).

[10] *Id.* at 744.

[11] *Id.* at 745-46.

[12] *Id.* at 747-48 (Stewart, J., dissenting).

[13] *Id.* at 749 (Marshall, J., dissenting).

[14] Under 50 U.S.C. § 1841(2), which cross references the definition in 18 U.S.C. § 3 127(3), the term "pen register" "means a device or process which records or decodes dialing, routing, addressing, or signaling information transmitted by an instrument or facility from which a wire or electronic communication is transmitted, provided, however, that such information shall not include the contents of any communication, but such term does not include any device or process used by a provider or customer of a wire or electronic communication service for billing, or recording as an incident to billing, for communications services provided by such provider or any device or process used by a provider or customer of a wire communication service for cost accounting or other like purposes in the ordinary course of its business."

[15] Under 50 U.S.C. § 1841(2), which cross references the definition in 18 U.S.C. § 3127(4), the term "trap and trace device" "means a device or process which captures the incoming electronic or other impulses which identify the originating number or other dialing, routing, addressing, and signaling information reasonably likely to identify the source of a wire or electronic communication, provided, however, that such information shall not include the contents of any communication."

[16] Under 50 U.S.C. § 1861, an investigation concerning a U.S. person may not be based solely on First Amendment protected activities.

[17] *See* CRS Report RL33320, *National Security Letters in Foreign Intelligence Investigations: Legal Background and Recent Amendments*, by Charles Doyle.

[18] Under 18 U.S.C. § 2709(f), "A library (as that term is defined in section 213(1) of the Library Services and Technology Act (20 U.S.C. 9 122(1)), the services of which include access to the Internet, books, journals, magazines, newspapers, or other similar forms of communication in print or digitally by patrons for their use, review, examination, or

circulation, is not a wire or electronic communication service provider for purposes of this section, unless the library is providing the services defined in section 2510(15) ("electronic communication service") of this title." Subsection (f) was added by P.L. 109-178, § 5.

[19] *See* CRS Report RL34409, *Selected Laws Governing the Disclosure of Customer Phone Records by Telecommunications Carriers*, by Kathleen Ann Ruane.

[20] Other provisions of this chapter deal with authorization for pen registers or trap and trace devices during emergencies, 50 U.S.C. § 1843, authorization during time of war, 50 U.S.C. 1844, use of information gathered under a FISA pen register or trap and trace device, 50 U.S.C. § 1845, and congressional oversight, 50 U.S.C. § 1846.

[21] Under 18 U.S.C. § 180 1(e), "foreign intelligence information" is defined to mean information that relates to, and if concerning a United States person is necessary to, the ability of the United States to protect against actual or potential attack or other grave hostile acts of a foreign power or an agent of a foreign power, sabotage or international terrorism by a foreign power or an agent of a foreign power, or clandestine intelligence activities by an intelligence service or network of a foreign power or by an agent of a foreign power; or information with respect to a foreign power or foreign territory that relates to, and if concerning a United States person is necessary to the national defense or the security of the United States or the conduct of the foreign affairs of the United States. The phrase "agents of a foreign power" currently includes, among others, non-U.S. persons that are engaged in international terrorism, but are not linked to an identifiable terrorist organization or foreign government. For a more detailed discussion of treatment of so-called "lone wolf" terrorists under FISA, *see* CRS Report R40138, *Amendments to the Foreign Intelligence Surveillance Act (FISA) Set to Expire February 28, 2010*, by Anna C. Henning and Edward C. Liu, at 2-4.

[22] Under 50 U.S.C. § 1801(i), "United States person" means a citizen of the United States, an alien lawfully admitted for permanent residence (as defined in section 1 101(a)(20) of Title 8), an unincorporated association a substantial number of members of which are citizens of the United States or aliens lawfully admitted for permanent residence, or a corporation which is incorporated in the United States, but does not include a corporation or an association which is a foreign power, as defined in subsection (a)(1), (2), or (3) of this section.

[23] P.L. 110-261, § 105.

[24] 18 U.S.C. § 3124 addresses assistance in installation and use of the pen register or trap and trace device; while 18 U.S.C. § 3125 deals with emergency installation of a pen register and trap or trap and trace device. 18 U.S.C. § 2136 provides for annual reports to Congress by the Attorney General on the number of applications by law enforcement agencies of the Department of Justice for pen registers or trap and trace devices orders, as well as certain details with respect to court orders issued in response to such applications.

[25] 50 U.S.C. § 186 1(b)(2)(A).

[26] The phrase "agents of a foreign power" currently includes, among others, non-U.S. persons that are engaged in international terrorism, but are not linked to an identifiable terrorist organization or foreign government. For a more detailed discussion of treatment of so-called "lone wolf" terrorists under FISA, *see* CRS Report R40138, *Amendments to the Foreign Intelligence Surveillance Act (FISA) Set to Expire February 28, 2010*, by Anna C. Henning and Edward C. Liu, at 2-4.

[27] 50 U.S.C. § 1861(c).

[28] A recipient of a FISA order under this section may disclose its existence to persons to whom disclosure is necessary to comply with the order, to an attorney to obtain legal advice with respect to the production of things in response to the order, as well as to other persons approved by the FBI. 50 U.S.C. § 1861(d)(1).

[29] 50 U.S.C. § 186 1(f)(2)(A).

[30] 50 U.S.C. § 186 1(f)(2)(B).

[31] 50 U.S.C. § 186 1(f)(2)(C)(i).

[32] 50 U.S.C. § 1861(f)(2)(C)(ii).

[33] *See* CRS Report R40138, *Amendments to the Foreign Intelligence Surveillance Act (FISA) Set to Expire February 28, 2010*, by Anna C. Henning and Edward C. Liu, at 7-11.

[34] This language was added by P.L. 109-177, Title I, § 107(b)(1)(B). It replaced an exception which covered "disclosure to a governmental entity if the provider reasonably believes that an emergency involving immediate danger of death or serious physical injury to any person justifies disclosure of the information."

[35] U.S. DEPARTMENT OF JUSTICE OFFICE OF THE INSPECTOR GENERAL, *A Review of the Federal Bureau of Investigation's Use of Exigent Letters and Other Informal Requests for Telephone Records*, at 260-263, 269 (Jan. 2010), available at http://www.justice.gov/oig/special/s1001r.pdf; U.S. DEPARTMENT OF JUSTICE, OFFICE OF THE INSPECTOR GENERAL, *A Review of the Federal Bureau of Investigation's Use of National Security Letters*, at 96 (March 2007), available at http://www.usdoj.gov/oig/special/s0703b/final.pdf.

[36] *Id.*

[37] *See* CRS Report RL33320, *National Security Letters in Foreign Intelligence Investigations: Legal Background and Recent Amendments*, by Charles Doyle.

[38] Under 18 U.S.C. § 2709(f), "A library (as that term is defined in section 213(1) of the Library Services and Technology Act (20 U.S.C. 9 122(1)), the services of which include access to the Internet, books, journals, magazines, newspapers, or other similar forms of communication in print or digitally by patrons for their use, review, examination, or circulation, is not a wire or electronic communication service provider for purposes of this section, unless the library is providing the services defined in section 2510(15) ("electronic communication service") of this title." Subsection (f) was added by P.L. 109-178, § 5.

[39] P.L. 109-177, § 116(a), rewrote subsection (c) of 18 U.S.C. § 2709, which formerly read, "No wire or electronic communication service provider, or officer, employee, or agent thereof, shall disclose to any person that the Federal Bureau of Investigation has sought or obtained access to information or records under this section." P.L. 109-178, § 4(b), rewrote subsection (c)(4), as amended by P.L. 109-177, § 116(a), which formerly read, "At the request of the Director of the Federal Bureau of Investigation or the designee of the Director, any person making or intending to make a disclosure under this section shall identify to the Director or such designee the person to whom such disclosure will be made or to whom such disclosure was made prior to the request, but in no circumstance shall a person be required to inform the Director or such designee that the person intends to consult an attorney to obtain legal advice or legal assistance."

[40] 47 U.S.C. § 222. Section 222 was added to the Communications Act by the Telecommunications Act of 1996. Telecommunications Act of 1996, P.L. 104-104, 110 Stat. 56 (codified at 47 U.S.C. §§ 151 et seq.).

[41] 47 U.S.C. § 222(h)(1).

[42] *See* FED. COMM. COMM'N, *Protecting Your Telephone Calling Records* (Oct. 20, 2008) available at http://www.fcc.gov/cgb/consumerfacts/phoneaboutyou.html.

[43] 47 U.S.C. § 222(h)(3).

[44] 47 U.S.C.§ 222(a).

[45] 47 U.S.C. § 222(b).

[46] 47 U.S.C. § 222(c)(1).

[47] 47 U.S.C. § 222(c)(2).

[48] 47 U.S.C. § 222(c)(3). The term "aggregate customer information" means collective data that relates to a group or category of services or customers, from which individual customer identities and characteristics have been removed. 47 U.S.C. § 222(h)(2).

[49] Whether the statutory provisions discussed in this report would fall within this exception is uncertain.

[50] 47 U.S.C. § 222(d).

[51] 47 U.S.C. § 222(e).

[52] *CPNI Order*, 13 FCC Rcd 8061.

[53] *U.S. West v. FCC*, 182 F.3d 1224 (10th Cir. 1999), *cert. denied Competition Policy Instit. v. U.S. West, Inc.*, 530 U.S. 1213 (2000).

[54] Except as required by law, carriers may not disclose CPNI to third parties or their own affiliates that do not provide communications-related services unless the consumer has given "opt in" consent, which is express written, oral, or electronic consent. 47 C.F.R. §§ 64.2005(b), 64.2007(b)(3); 64.2008(e); see also 47 C.F.R. § 64.2003(h) (defining "opt- in approval").

[55] 47 C.F.R. §§ 64.2005(b), 64.2007(b)(1).

[56] FCC Consumer Advisory: Protecting the Privacy of Your Telephone Calling Records, at http://www.fcc.gov/cgb/ consumerfacts/phoneaboutyou.html.

[57] 47 C.F.R. §§ 64.2008.

[58] 47 C.F.R. §§ 64.2009.

[59] 47 C.F.R. §§ 64.2009(e).

[60] In the Matter of Cbeyond Communications, LLC, 2006 FCC LEXIS 1902 (April 21, 2006), at http://www.fcc.gov/ eb/Orders/2006/DA-06-916A1 .html.

[61] *See* CRS Report RL34409, *Selected Laws Governing the Disclosure of Customer Phone Records by Telecommunications Carriers*, by Kathleen Ann Ruane, at 9.

[62] 47 U.S.C. § 502.

[63] 47 U.S.C. § 503(b)(1).

[64] FCC Forfeiture Proceedings, Limits on the amount of forfeiture assessed, 47 C.F.R. Part 1.80(b).

In: The Fourth Amendment
Editors: Jesse V. Kessler

ISBN: 978-1-61728-885-2

Chapter 4

HERRING V. UNITED STATES: EXTENSION OF THE GOOD-FAITH EXCEPTION TO THE EXCLUSIONARY RULE IN FOURTH AMENDMENT CASES

Anna C. Henning

SUMMARY

The Fourth Amendment to the U.S. Constitution provides a right against "unreasonable searches and seizures." To deter the federal and state governments from violating this right, courts have developed an "exclusionary rule," which requires that evidence obtained as a result of an invalid search or seizure be excluded from use at trial.

The Supreme Court has narrowed the scope of the exclusionary rule in several cases since the late 1970s. In *United States v. Leon*, the Court created the "good-faith" exception to the exclusionary rule. The good-faith exception applies when officers conduct a search or seizure with "objectively reasonable reliance" on, for example, a warrant that is not obviously invalid but that a judicial magistrate should not have signed.

Until a 2006 case, *Hudson v. Michigan*, the Supreme Court had applied the good-faith exception only in cases in which the error creating the constitutional violation was caused by judicial or legislative actors, rather than by the police themselves. In *Hudson*, the Court applied the exception to a case in which police officers had violated the "knock and announce" rule by entering a home without waiting a sufficient period of time.

In *Herring v. United States*, a 2009 decision, the Supreme Court for the first time applied the good-faith exception to bar application of the exclusionary rule in a case involving police error regarding a warrant. A police officer in the case mistakenly identified an arrest warrant for the defendant. The Court held that evidence discovered after the subsequent arrest was admissible at trial because the officer's error was not "deliberate" and the officers involved were not "culpable."

In future cases, courts will apply the *Herring* "deliberate and culpable" test to determine whether to admit evidence obtained as a result of a search or seizure which is unconstitutional as a consequence of police error. A second impact of the *Herring* decision is a weaker constitutional footing for the exclusionary rule. Whereas judicially-created remedies have gained "constitutional status" in the context of some other constitutional rights, it appears that the exclusionary rule lacks such a grounding under the Court's current Fourth Amendment jurisprudence.

INTRODUCTION

The U.S. Supreme Court recognized in 1803 that in order to maintain a society governed by laws, a legal remedy should accompany each legal right.[1] Toward this end, courts apply various remedies to ensure effective enforcement of constitutional rights. For example, courts sometimes order retrials to remedy violations of defendants' trial-by-jury or assistance-of-counsel rights.

A remedy that excludes impermissibly obtained evidence from use at a criminal trial – the "exclusionary rule" – similarly protects constitutional rights. The exclusionary rule typically applies in cases involving violations by law enforcement of rights guaranteed by the Fourth or Fifth Amendments to the U.S. Constitution.[2] It differs from remedies such as retrial, because in addition to retrospectively redressing injustice, its major aim is prospective deterrence of government misconduct. In theory, although it only actually redresses violations when probative evidence is found, the exclusionary rule also protects innocent people by deterring unwarranted privacy intrusions.

The rule operates to prohibit the introduction at trial of probative evidence that would be admissible if collected in a constitutionally permissible manner. Because the excluded evidence is frequently incriminating, many believe that its application aids criminals in escaping punishment. For this reason, the rule has long been controversial. In past cases, the Supreme Court has defended the rule as a necessary corollary to the constitutional rights it protects.[3] More recently, a division has emerged. Some justices adhere to the view of the rule as constitutionally required. Other justices express concerns about the cost to society of freeing criminals who would likely be convicted if the excluded evidence was admitted.

Over the past several decades, the Supreme Court has narrowed the scope of the exclusionary rule in Fourth Amendment cases – that is, in cases involving illegal searches or seizures. The Court's 2009 decision in *Herring v. United States* furthers this trend.[4] Because *Herring* is the first Supreme Court decision that rejects the exclusionary rule in the context of police error regarding a warrant, the decision has made news headlines and prompted debate about whether the *Herring* decision appropriately limits the exclusionary rule's reach.[5]

Overview of the Fourth Amendment and the Exclusionary Rule

The Fourth Amendment to the U.S. Constitution provides a right "of the people to be secure in their persons, houses, papers, and effects, against unreasonable searches and seizures."[6] As a general rule, "reasonableness" requires law enforcement officers to demonstrate "probable cause" and obtain a warrant (unless a recognized warrant exception applies) before conducting searches or seizures.[7] For example, under the general rule, a police officer may not arrest a person unless a judicial magistrate has issued a warrant, based on evidence establishing sufficient probable cause, for that person's arrest. Likewise, a police officer typically may not search a person's belongings without first obtaining a warrant that describes, with sufficient particularity, the property for which sufficient evidence justifies a search.

The Constitution does not explicitly provide a remedy that applies when governmental actors violate a citizen's Fourth Amendment right.[8] To deter Fourth Amendment violations, courts apply the exclusionary rule, which "is often the only remedy effective to redress a Fourth Amendment violation."[9] In the Fourth Amendment context, the exclusionary rule requires a trial court to forbid the prosecution's use of evidence obtained as a result of an unconstitutional search or seizure.[10] For example, if a police officer arrests a person in violation of constitutionally mandated procedures (i.e., without a warrant or a warrant exception), then the exclusionary rule requires a trial court to suppress any contraband the officer discovered during the search incident to that arrest.

Although the exclusionary rule protects constitutional rights, a question remains regarding its status – i.e., is it constitutionally required in the Fourth Amendment context? In past Fourth Amendment cases, the Supreme Court has stated that the exclusionary rule is "of constitutional origin."[11] In other cases, the Court has characterized the rule as a "judicially created remedy ... *rather than* a personal constitutional right."[12] This distinction affects Congress' authority to alter the exclusionary rule statutorily. Congress may not reduce a constitutionally guaranteed remedy but could potentially alter a rule that lacks constitutional status.

Regardless, the Court has narrowed the exclusionary rule's reach in Fourth Amendment cases throughout the past several decades. For example, it has barred courts' use of the rule in civil cases, grand jury proceedings, and parole revocation hearings. Arguably, the most important narrowing trend has been the Court's development of the good-faith exception.

The Good-Faith Exception

The Supreme Court introduced what has come to be known as the good-faith exception in *United States v. Leon.* [13] In *Leon*, the Court held that the exclusionary rule does not apply when police officers act with "objectively reasonable reliance" on a search warrant later found to be invalid.[14] Language in the opinion embraced a cautionary "balancing" approach to the exclusionary rule in which the benefits of exclusion (namely any deterrence effect on unconstitutional police action) must outweigh the costs (namely the risk that a guilty person will escape justice because evidence is excluded at trial) before the Court will apply the rule to new factual circumstances.[15]

Police officers in *Leon*, acting on a tip about drug activity in a particular home, investigated the license plate number and connections of a man who exited the home holding a small paper sack.[16] The officers then observed people coming and going from the residences of several people connected to that man, including the home of Leon, the respondent in the case, whom the man had listed as his employer and who had a criminal record.[17] Based on these observations, the officers obtained a warrant from a magistrate to search three homes and several automobiles.[18] The subsequent search uncovered illegal drugs and other evidence.[19]

At trial, a federal district court held that the warrant was not supported by probable cause; thus, the search violated the Fourth Amendment.[20] Applying the exclusionary rule remedy, the district court suppressed the evidence of drugs found in the homes and cars.[21] On appeal, the Supreme Court held that suppression is inappropriate in cases, such as *Leon*, where the violation occurred despite a police officer's "objectively reasonable reliance" – for example, on a warrant that is actually invalid.[22]

By creating an exception to the exclusionary rule, the *Leon* court arguably opened the door to permitting evidence in cases involving multiple types of Fourth Amendment violations. However, the *Leon* decision itself addressed only the particular circumstance in which a warrant exists but was invalidly issued based on insufficient probable cause. The *Leon* opinion, including several exceptions to the good-faith exception articulated in the case, evidences a holding that only addresses that particular context.[23]

To justify its holding, the *Leon* court noted the logical inconsistency between exclusion in cases involving non-police errors and the rule's traditional deterrence rationale, stating: "Penalizing the officer for the magistrate's error, rather than his own, cannot logically contribute to the deterrence of Fourth Amendment violations."[24] Based on the Court's reliance on this rationale, one might argue that the Court did not originally anticipate an extension of the good-faith exception to cases involving police error.

The Supreme Court has extended the *Leon* good-faith exception in relatively minor ways over the past several decades. In a 1995 case, *Illinois v. Krull*, the Court applied the exception where police officers had searched an auto dealer's list of licenses pursuant to a statute that courts later struck down as unconstitutional.[25] Several years later, in *Arizona v. Evans*, the Court applied *Leon* to evidence obtained after an arrest based on a facially valid warrant that the clerk of the court had neglected to show had been quashed seventeen days earlier.[26]

Until recently, these extensions had involved police reliance on errors made by actors – for example, the clerk of the court in *Evans* and the legislative branch in *Krull* – not the police themselves. Furthermore, in a 2004 case, *Groh v. Ramirez*, the Court seemed to draw an explicit line between police errors and errors made by other actors.[27] Police officers in *Groh* searched a home where they suspected that the owners had stored illegal weaponry.[28] The court of appeals held that the search warrant, which a magistrate had signed but the officers had themselves prepared, violated the constitutional requirement that property to be searched be described with particularity; thus, the officers' search violated the homeowners' Fourth Amendment rights.[29] On appeal, the Supreme Court declined to apply the good-faith exception to the exclusionary rule, because it found that the officers' search pursuant to a warrant that failed to list property to be searched was not a "reasonable" mistake.[30] In so holding, the Court stressed that the officer in *Groh* was himself responsible for the Fourth Amendment violation.[31]

However, only two years after *Groh*, the Court declined to find any distinction between police error and third-party errors. In *Michigan v. Hudson*, it held that police officers' violation of the "knock and announce" rule did not trigger the exclusionary rule.[32] Knock and announce, an "ancient" procedure derived from common-law, constitutional, and statutory sources, protects occupants' privacy by requiring police officers to wait a short while after knocking and announcing their presence before entering a residence for which they have a warrant.[33] The rule is viewed as a less stringent requirement than the warrant or probable cause requirements under the Fourth Amendment, and the *Hudson* court noted that it is "unnecessary" in various circumstances.[34] Because the Court limited its opinion in *Hudson* to knock and announce violations, it was unclear after that case whether the Court would extend the good-faith exception to more serious police errors, such as those involving warrants or warrant exceptions.

HERRING V. UNITED STATES

In *Herring v. United States*, a 2009 case, the Supreme Court for the first time applied the good- faith exception in a case involving police error regarding a warrant.[35] Officers arrested the defendant, Bennie Dean Herring, outside of an impound lot where Herring had come to retrieve an item from his truck.[36] An officer at the lot, recognizing Herring, called the county warrant clerk to determine whether an outstanding arrest warrant applied to him.[37] The warrant clerk found no such warrant but agreed to inquire about warrants in a neighboring county.[38] The clerk then identified as active an arrest warrant in the neighboring county, although it was in fact no longer active.[39] After learning about the warrant, two officers followed Herring from the impound lot, arrested him, and performed a search incident to arrest.[40] The officers discovered methamphetamine in Herring's pocket and an illegal pistol in his vehicle.[41]

Because the arrest warrant was actually invalid, both parties in *Herring* admitted that a Fourth Amendment violation had occurred.[42] The disagreement in the case centered on whether the exclusionary rule should apply to suppress the evidence obtained as a result of the violation.[43] Extending the good-faith exception, the Court held that the exclusionary rule should not apply.[44]

The Court also announced a new test for the exception: "To trigger the exclusionary rule," police conduct must be "sufficiently deliberate" and the police must be "sufficiently culpable."[45] The Court emphasized that this "analysis of deliberateness and culpability" is objective: a court should ascertain not whether the police officer in question acted with good intentions, but rather "'whether a reasonably well trained officer would have known that the search was illegal' in light of 'all the circumstances.'"[46]

In rejecting the exclusionary rule in *Herring*, the Court appeared to embrace the view that it is not constitutionally required in the Fourth Amendment context. Quoting *Hudson v. Michigan*, the Court emphasized that the exclusionary rule is a "'last resort'" rather than a "necessary consequence of a Fourth Amendment violation."[47] It then applied a cost-benefit analysis similar to the approach in *Leon*, stating that in order for the exclusionary rule to apply, "the benefits of deterrence must outweigh the costs."[48]

In contrast, dissenting justices in *Herring* cited cases in which the Court has viewed the exclusionary rule as "inseparable" from the Fourth Amendment, suggesting that the remedy of exclusion has constitutional status.[49] Starting from this different philosophical foundation, the dissenters rejected the cost-benefit approach as inappropriate and would instead have applied the exclusionary rule in all cases where it has "*any power* to discourage" law enforcement misconduct.[50] Dissenters also highlighted the substantive distinction between errors made by judicial branch personnel and errors made by police, noting three specific distinctions: (1) the exclusionary rule historically aims to deter police, rather than judicial, misconduct; (2) no evidence suggests that court employees are "inclined to subvert the Fourth Amendment"; and (3) because judicial officers have no stake in the outcome of particular criminal investigations, "there [is] 'no basis for believing that application of the exclusionary rule ... [would] have a significant effect on court employees.'"[51] For those reasons, the four dissenting justices would not have extended the good-faith exception to situations involving police conduct regarding a warrant.

LEGAL IMPLICATIONS

Although the *Herring* decision broadens the good-faith exception to the exclusionary rule and has shifted the analysis to one of "deliberateness and culpability," the scope of its impact remains to be seen. For example, although it is perhaps difficult to imagine recordkeeping errors that would meet the Court's "deliberate and culpable" test, the *Herring* court suggested that "reckless[ness] in maintaining a warrant system," such as a recordkeeping system that routinely led to false arrests, could justify application of the exclusionary rule.[52] Thus, although most recordkeeping and clerical errors made by police will no doubt fit within the relatively broad parameters of the good-faith exception as interpreted in *Herring*, lower courts will likely decline to apply *Herring* in situations where defendants demonstrate knowledge or ongoing patterns of wrongdoing by law enforcement officers.

In addition to broadening the good-faith exception, the *Herring* decision appears to further the trend toward interpreting the exclusionary rule as lacking constitutional status. One important outcome of this might be greater congressional authority to legislate changes to the Fourth Amendment exclusionary rule. Congress has occasionally considered legislation that would expand or contract the exclusionary rule's reach.[53] Because Congress may always guarantee a greater right than the Constitution demands as a minimum, Congress clearly may expand the remedy of exclusion. In contrast, whether Congress has the authority to restrict the remedy of exclusion depends upon the status of the remedy vis-à-vis the Constitution. If, as *Herring* appears to indicate, the exclusionary rule lacks constitutional status, then legislation restricting the right – for example, legislation expanding the *Herring* holding – is likely constitutionally permissible. If, on the other hand, the exclusionary rule is a constitutionally required remedy in Fourth Amendment cases, as the *Herring* dissenters suggested, then Congress would lack the authority to narrow the scope of the remedy.

Author Contact Information

Anna C. Henning
Legislative Attorney
ahenning@crs.loc.gov, 7-4067

End Notes

[1] *See Marbury v. Madison*, 5 U.S. 137, 163 (1803).

[2] The exclusionary rule is sometimes designated as the "Fifth Amendment exclusionary rule" or the "Fourth Amendment exclusionary rule." This report addresses only the Fourth Amendment context. As applied to the Fifth Amendment, the rule typically bars the prosecution's use of evidence obtained as a result of coercive interrogation techniques proscribed by the Fifth Amendment's self-incrimination or due-process clauses.

[3] *See, e.g., Mapp v. Ohio*, 367 U.S. 643, 649 (1961).

[4] 555 U.S. __ (2009).

[5] *See, e.g.*, David Stout, *Justices Say Evidence is Valid Despite Police Error*, NY Times A4 (Jan. 15, 2009); Adam Liptak, *Justices Ease Limits on Evidence*, NY Times A17 (Jan. 15, 2009) (Late Ed. (East Coast)).

[6] U.S. Const. Amend. IV.

[7] *See, e.g., Atwater v. City of Lago Vista*, 532 U.S. 318, 354 (2001) (recognizing a warrant exception for arrest of an individual who commits a crime in an officer's presence, as long as the arrest is supported by probable cause). Probable cause is "a fluid concept – turning on the assessment of probabilities in particular factual contexts." *Illinois v. Gates*, 462 U.S. 213, 232 (1983). For example, for issuance of a search warrant, probable cause requires an issuing magistrate to determine, based on specific evidence, whether there exists a "fair probability" that, for example, an area contains contraband. *Id.* at 238. Exceptions to the warrant requirement include, for example, "exigent circumstances" where people's lives are at risk or illegal items in "plain view" during a search authorized for other items.

[8] In a 1961 case, *Mapp v. Ohio*, 367 U.S. 643 (1961), the Supreme Court held that the due process clause of the Fourteenth Amendment to the U.S. Constitution incorporated the Fourth Amendment to the states. Thus, the Fourth Amendment prohibits unreasonable searches and seizures by state and local, in addition to federal, governments.

[9] *Herring*, 555 U.S. __, Slip. op. at 6. (Ginsburg, J., dissenting) (citing *Mapp*, 367 U.S. at 652).

[10] Although it was not termed the "exclusionary rule" until later, the Supreme Court first clearly articulated a remedy of excluding evidence as a result of Fourth Amendment violations in *Weeks v. United States*. 232 U.S. 383, 393 (1914) ("If letters and private documents can thus be seized and held and used in evidence against a citizen accused of an offense, the protection of the Fourth Amendment ... is of no value"). In *Weeks*, the Court implied that the exclusionary rule is grounded in long-standing judicial precedent. *Id.* at 398 ("That papers wrongfully seized should be turned over to the accused has been frequently recognized in the early as well as later decisions of the courts.") It also suggested that the rule is constitutionally required. *Id.* (stating that the lower court had violated the defendant's constitutional rights by declining to apply the rule). Although the *Weeks* holding applied only to evidence obtained by federal officers, the Court later applied the rule to the states in *Mapp v. Ohio*. 367 U.S. at 655.

[11] *Mapp*, 367 U.S. at 649. In *Mapp*, the Court relied on the exclusionary rule's constitutional status to hold that the Fourteenth Amendment had incorporated the rule to the states. *Id.* at 655. Although in theory, this application to the states loses its legal foundation if the rule lacks constitutional status, states have generally continued to apply the rule to the extent that the federal courts have required it, despite the Court's recent suggestions that the remedy is not constitutionally required.

[12] *See, e.g., United States v. Calandra*, 414 U.S. 338, 348 (1974) (emphasis added). The Court's reliance on the rule's "judicially-created" status in concluding that the Fourth Amendment exclusionary rule lacks constitutional status contrasts with the Court's approach in other areas of constitutional interpretation. For example, in the Fifth Amendment context, the Court has recognized that the so-called "*Miranda* warnings," and their exclusionary-rule corollary, are a judicially-created rule aimed to deter police conduct. Nonetheless, in

Dickerson v. United States, the Court held that the *Miranda* warnings have the status of constitutional interpretation; thus, Congress cannot eliminate the *Miranda* warnings requirement by statute. 530 U.S. 428, 434-435 (2000).

[13] 468 U.S. 897 (1984).

[14] *Id.* at 922.

[15] *Id.* at 909-13.

[16] *Id.* at 901-02.

[17] *Id.*

[18] *Id.*

[19] *Id.* at 902.

[20] *Id.* at 903.

[21] *Id.* at 903-04.

[22] *Id.* at 923. Despite its emphasis on the police officer's "good faith," the operative language in *Leon* focuses not on the officer's subjective integrity, but rather on whether the officer's reliance on the defective warrant was "objectively reasonable." *Id.* at 903-04, 923.

[23] The *Leon* court articulated four exceptions to its holding, in which this good-faith exception would not apply: (1) no reasonable officer would have relied on the affidavit underlying the warrant; (2) the warrant is defective on its face for failing to state the place to be searched or things to be seized; (3) the warrant was obtained by fraud on the part of a government official; or (4) the magistrate issuing the warrant had "wholly abandoned his judicial role." *Id.* at 923.

[24] *Id.* at 921.

[25] 480 U.S. 340, 349-50 (1987).

[26] 514 U.S. 1 (1995).

[27] 540 U.S. 551 (2004).

[28] *Id.* at 554-55.

[29] *Id.* at 556.

[30] *Id.* at 563 ("Given that the particularity requirement is set forth in the text of the Constitution, no reasonable officer could believe that a warrant that plainly did not comply with that requirement was valid.")

[31] *See, e.g., Id.* at 564 ("... because petitioner himself prepared the invalid warrant, he may not argue that he reasonably relied on the Magistrate's assurance that the warrant contained an adequate description of the things to be seized and was therefore valid.").

[32] 547 U.S. 586 (2006). For a more detailed analysis of the *Hudson v. Michigan* decision, see CRS Report RS22475, *Hudson v. Michigan: The Exclusionary Rule's Applicability to "Knock-and-Announce" Violations*, by Alison M. Smith.

[33] *Hudson*, 547 at 589-90.

[34] *Id.* at 590. Despite this argument, the decision was not without impact. Dissenting justices in *Hudson* argued that the decision "weakens" and possibly even "destroys" the knock-and-announce rule. *Id.* at 605 (Breyer, J., dissenting).

[35] 555 U.S. __.

[36] *Id.*, Slip op. at 2.

[37] *Id.*

[38] *Id.*

[39] *Id.*

[40] *Id.*

[41] *Id.*

[42] *Herring*, slip op. at 4.

[43] *Id.*

[44] Slip op. at 9.

[45] *Id.*

[46] Slip op. at 10 (quoting *Leon*, 468 U.S. at 922 n.23).

[47] Slip op. at 5 (quoting *Hudson v. Michigan*, 547 U.S. 586, 591 (2006)).

[48] Slip op. at 6.
[49] Slip op. at 5 (Ginsburg, J., dissenting) (citing, among others, *Whiteley v. Warden, Wyo. State Penitentiary*, 401 U.S. 560, 568-69 (1971)).
[50] *See* Slip op. at 1 (Ginsburg, J., dissenting).
[51] Slip op. at 1 (Breyer, J., dissenting) (quoting *Evans*, 514 U.S. at 15).
[52] Slip op. at 11.
[53] For example, legislation introduced in 1995 attempted to codify the good-faith exception by removing the remedy of exclusion in federal courts in cases in which police officers had acted in good faith. Exclusionary Rule Reform Act of 1995, H.R. 666, 104th Cong. (1995).

In: The Fourth Amendment
Editors: Jesse V. Kessler
ISBN: 978-1-61728-885-2

Chapter 5

FOURTH AMENDMENT PROTECTIONS AGAINST STUDENT STRIP SEARCHES: *SAFFORD UNIFIED SCHOOL DISTRICT #1 V. REDDING*

David H. Carpenter

SUMMARY

The Fourth Amendment protects individuals from unreasonable searches and seizures. What a court determines to be "reasonable" depends on the nature of the search and its underlying governmental purpose.

This report provides an analysis of the U.S. Supreme Court's 2009 decision, *Safford Unified School District #1 v. Redding*, which addressed the constitutionality of a strip search of a 13-yearold middle school student. Based on the facts of the case, the Court held that the school's search of a student's book bag and outer clothing was in accordance with the Fourth Amendment. However, as a result of a number of factual deficiencies, the search became constitutionally unreasonable when it went beyond the student's outerwear and ultimately led to the student being required to shake and pull out her bra and underwear.

For a discussion of drug testing in public schools, see CRS Report RL34624, *Governmental Drug Testing Programs: Legal and Constitutional Developments*, by David H. Carpenter.

INTRODUCTION

The Fourth Amendment to the U.S. Constitution protects individuals from unreasonable searches and seizures. What a court determines to be "reasonable" depends on the nature of the search and its underlying governmental purpose. This report provides an analysis of the U.S. Supreme Court's 2009 decision, *Safford Unified School District #1 v. Redding*,[1] which addressed the strip search of a 13-year-old middle school student.[2]

FACTS OF THE CASE

In October 2003, Savana Redding was a 13-year-old student at Safford Middle School. At the time, Kerry Wilson was Safford Middle School's assistant principal. Wilson confiscated four prescription strength ibuprofen, a single over-the-counter naproxen pain reliever, and a day planner from another student, Marissa Glines. Inside the day planner were multiple knives and lighters, and a cigarette. Glines indicated that she had received the pills and the day planner from Redding. The pills were not allowed on school premises without prior approval.[3] A week prior to this incident, a different student told Wilson that students were carrying weapons on the school premises and dealing pills, and that he had become ill after taking a pill that he had received from a classmate.[4]

Wilson ordered Redding into his office and showed her the day planner with the contraband inside. Redding admitted that the planner was hers, but said that she had allowed Glines to borrow it a few days before. Redding denied ownership of the knives, lighters, and cigarette that were in the planner. Wilson then asked Redding about the pills and informed her that he had been told that Redding had been distributing these pills to other students. Redding told Wilson that she did not know anything about the pills and denied distributing them to others. Wilson then asked if he could search through Redding's book bag, which Redding allowed. A female assistant and Wilson searched the bag, but did not find any prohibited items. Wilson then ordered

Redding to go to the nurse's office for the nurse and female assistant to search Redding's clothes for other pills. The two female school employees searched her outerwear and eventually had Redding remove her clothes down to her bra and underwear, at which point they required Redding "to pull her bra out and to the side and shake it, and to pull out the elastic on her underpants, thus exposing her breasts and pelvic area to some degree." During the conduct of this search, the employees found no pills.[5]

Redding's mother subsequently sued the school and the three school employees involved, claiming they violated Redding's Fourth Amendment rights against unreasonable searches and seizures.

HOLDING AND LEGAL REASONING

Eight justices held that the search resulted in a violation of Savana Redding's Fourth Amendment rights.[6]

Generally speaking, the government is required by the Fourth Amendment to obtain warrants based on probable cause in order to effectuate constitutional searches and seizures.[7] An exception to ordinary warrant requirements has radually evolved, however, for cases where a "special need" of the government, unrelated to criminal law enforcement, is found by the courts to outweigh any "diminished expectation" of privacy invaded by a search. Even in circumstances where warrantless searches are permitted, they ordinarily "must be based on 'probable cause' to believe that a violation of the law has occurred."[8] Nevertheless, the Supreme Court has determined that neither a warrant nor probable cause is invariably required. In such situations, a Fourth Amendment standard based on a balancing test has been crafted by the Court. This "special needs" approach appears to confer optimal power on the government to search where "compelling" reason exists and correspondingly warrants less protection to the individual's "diminished expectation of privacy."

In *New Jersey v. T.L. O.*, the Court found that students are one group of individuals which has a "diminished expectation of privacy."[9] In that case, the Court held that, for searches conducted by school officials in the school setting, "a careful balancing of governmental and private interests suggests that the public interest is best served by a Fourth Amendment standard of reasonableness that stops short of probable cause."[10] The Court went on to apply a "reasonable suspicion" standard for such a search and stated "[a search] will be permissible in its scope when the measures adopted are reasonably related to the objectives of the search and not excessively intrusive in light of the age and sex of the student and the nature of the infraction."[11]

To determine if there is reasonable suspicion to warrant a school search, the courts generally look to three different factors: (1) "the degree to which known facts imply prohibited conduct"; (2) "the specificity of the information received"; and (3) "the reliability of its source."[12] However, these factors "do not rigidly control," rather they are "fluid concepts that take their substantive content from the particular contexts in which they are being assessed."[13] The Court went on:

> Perhaps the best that can be said generally about the required knowledge component of probable cause for a law enforcement officer's evidence search is that it raise a 'fair probability' or a 'substantial chance' of discovering evidence of criminal activity. The lesser standard for school searches could as readily be described as a moderate chance of finding evidence of wrongdoing.[14]

Applying these standards, the Court held that the school's search of Redding's book bag and outer clothing was in accordance with the Fourth Amendment. The school had reasonable suspicion Redding was involved in pill distribution as a result of Gline's possession of banned pills; Gline's accusation of Redding; Redding's acknowledged ownership of the day planner; and circumstantial evidence that Redding had been involved in alcohol consumption and cigarette smoking at a school dance a month or two before. Additionally, the search of Redding's book bag and outer clothing were conducted in "relative privacy ... and [were] not excessively intrusive...."[15]

The search became constitutionally unreasonable when it went beyond Redding's outerwear and ultimately led to Redding being required to shake and pull out her bra and underwear. The fact that the two school employees present testified that they did not see Redding's private areas was immaterial to the Court.[16] It stated:

> The very fact of [Redding's] pulling her underwear away from her body in the presence of the two officials who were able to see her necessarily exposed her breasts and pelvic area to some degree, and both subjective and reasonable societal expectations of personal privacy support the treatment of such a search as categorically distinct, requiring distinct elements of justification on the part of the school authorities....[17]

Redding's subjective belief that the search was scary and humiliating was reasonable, as it was "consistent [with] the experiences of other young people similarly searched, whose adolescent vulnerability intensifies the patent intrusiveness of the exposure."[18]

In addition, Wilson knew that the pills found on Glines were common pain relievers, the strongest of which were equivalent to two Advil. There was no indication that the pills were being distributed in mass quantities or that single students were receiving a large number of pills. Additionally, there was no evidence supporting the belief that Redding was hiding pills in her underwear.[19]

Thus, the Court concluded, "[w]e think that the combination of these deficiencies was fatal to finding the search reasonable."[20] The Safford Court makes clear that, while students enjoy diminished privacy expectations and school administrators have a lower level of suspicion to eclipse, there are limits to when and how searches may be conducted in the school setting. However, ascertaining if a school administrator has encroached upon those constitutional limits will depend largely on the facts of the case.

Author Contact Information

David H. Carpenter
Legislative Attorney
dcarpenter@crs.loc.gov, 7-9118

End Notes

[1] 557 U.S. ___, 1-2 (2009).

[2] For a discussion of drug testing in public schools, see CRS Report RL34624, *Governmental Drug Testing Programs: Legal and Constitutional Developments*, by David H. Carpenter.

[3] *Id.*

[4] *Id* at 5.

[5] *Id.* at 1-2.

[6] *Id.* at 1. Eight justices found the search unconstitutional, with Justice Thomas as the lone dissenter. However, Justices Stevens and Ginsburg dissented from the majority on the question of whether Wilson, the assistant principal, warranted qualified immunity for the search. "A school official is entitled to qualified immunity where clearly established law does not show that the search violated the Fourth Amendment. *Id.* at 11 (internal citations and quotations omitted).

[7] Camara v. Municipal Court, 387 U.S. 523, 528-29 (1967) ("one governing principle, justified by history and by current experience, has consistently been followed: except in certain

carefully defined classes of cases, a search of private property without proper consent is 'unreasonable' unless it has been authorized by a valid search warrant.").

[8] New Jersey v. T.L.O., 469 U.S. 325, 340 (1985).

[9] *Id.*

[10] *Id.* at 341.

[11] *Id.* at 342.

[12] *Safford*, 557 U.S. at 4 (internal citations omitted).

[13] *Id.* (internal citations and quotations omitted).

[14] *Id.* at 4-5 (internal citations and quotations omitted).

[15] *Id.* at 7.

[16] *Id.* at 8.

[17] *Id.* (internal citations and quotations omitted).

[18] *Id.*

[19] *Id.* at 9-10.

[20] *Id.* at 10.

In: The Fourth Amendment
Editors: Jesse V. Kessler

ISBN: 978-1-61728-885-2

Chapter 6

GOVERNMENTAL DRUG TESTING PROGRAMS: LEGAL AND CONSTITUTIONAL DEVELOPMENTS

David H. Carpenter
American Law Division

SUMMARY

Constitutional law on the subject of governmentally mandated drug testing is primarily an outgrowth of the Fourth Amendment prohibition on unreasonable searches and seizures. Judicial exceptions to traditional requirements of a warrant and individualized suspicion for "administrative" searches have been extended to random drug testing of public employees and school students where the government is able to demonstrate a "special need" beyond the demands of ordinary law enforcement. In the public employment setting, however, special needs analysis has largely been confined to relatively narrow circumstances directly implicating "compelling" public safety, law enforcement, or national security interests of the government. More generalized governmental concerns for the "integrity" or efficient operation of the public workplace have usually not been deemed sufficient to justify interference with the "reasonable expectation of privacy" of workers or other individuals to be tested. Additionally, warrantless, suspicionless drug testing programs that serve primarily a criminal law enforcement purpose are likely to be unconstitutional.

The constitutional parameters of "special needs" analysis is outlined in a series of Supreme Court rulings. In *Skinner v. Railway Labor Executives Association*, the U.S. Supreme Court upheld post-accident drug and alcohol testing of railway employees after major train accidents or incidents, and it approved the testing of U.S. Customs employees seeking promotion to certain "sensitive" jobs involving firearms use, drug interdiction duties, or access to classified information in *National Treasury Employees Union v. Von Raab*. These decisions established that "compelling" governmental interests in public safety or national security may, in appropriate circumstances, override constitutional objections to testing procedures by employees whose privacy expectations are diminished by the nature of their duties or workplace scrutiny to which they are otherwise subject. In *Veronia School District v. Acton*, the Supreme Court first approved of random drug testing procedures for high school student athletes, a holding that was subsequently extended, in *Board of Education of Independent School District No. 92 of Pottawatomie County v. Earls*, to permit random drug testing of students participating in non-athletic extracurricular activities. However, the Court placed limitations on the "special needs" doctrine when, in *Chandler v. Miller*, it voided a Georgia law requiring drug testing of candidates for state office for lack of a governmental need substantial enough to warrant suspicionless searches. Additionally, the Court generally has struck down drug testing policies that primarily serve criminal law enforcement purposes, such as in *Ferguson v. City of Charleston*.

INTRODUCTION

One outgrowth of the nation's "war on drugs" has been a proliferation of governmental initiatives at the federal, state, and local levels to detect and deter illegal drug use in the workplace, the schools, and by recipients of public benefits. Since the late 1 980s, the federal government has conducted "random" drug tests of executive branch employees in "sensitive" job positions and has implemented similar procedures for public and private employees in transportation and other safety or security-related industries. Aiding these efforts are state and local governmental testing programs for police officers, firefighters, prison guards, teachers, and other personnel with public safety responsibilities. Beyond employment, states and localities have required other individuals to submit to drug testing, such as students in public schools.

Constitutional challenges to "suspicionless" or random governmental drug testing most often focus on issues of personal privacy and Fourth Amendment protections against "unreasonable" searches and seizures. Generally speaking, the government is required by the Fourth Amendment to obtain warrants based on probable cause in order to effectuate constitutional searches and seizures. An exception to ordinary warrant requirements has gradually evolved, however, for cases where a "special need" of the government, not related to criminal law enforcement, is found by the courts to outweigh any "diminished expectation" of privacy invaded by a search.

In 1989, the U.S. Supreme Court upheld post-accident drug and alcohol testing of railway employees after major train accidents or incidents, in *Skinner v. Railway Labor Executives Association*,[1] and of U.S. Customs employees seeking promotion to certain "sensitive" jobs involving firearms use, drug interdiction duties, or access to classified information, in *National Treasury Employees Union v. Von Raab*.[2] These rulings make clear that "compelling" governmental interests in public safety or national security may, in appropriate circumstances, override constitutional objections to testing procedures by employees whose privacy expectations are diminished by the nature of their duties or the workplace scrutiny to which they are otherwise subject. In *Veronia School District v. Acton*,[3] the Supreme Court first approved of random drug testing procedures — for high school student athletes rather than public employees — after it had earlier left standing lower court decisions allowing for certain suspicionless testing of police officers,[4] transit employees,[5] nuclear power plant employees,[6] Justice Department lawyers who hold top-secret security clearances,[7] and Army civilian drug counselors.[8] *Veronia* was subsequently extended by the Court to permit random drug testing of students participating in nonathletic extracurricular activities.[9] However, the Court distinguished earlier rulings when, in *Chandler v. Miller*,[10] it voided a Georgia law requiring drug testing of candidates for state office because no "special need" substantial enough to warrant suspicionless searches was shown. Additionally, the Court generally has struck down drug testing policies that primarily serve criminal law enforcement purposes, such as in *Ferguson v. City of Charleston*.

There are no federal constitutional limits on the ability of private employers or other non-public entities to conduct drug tests. The Fourth Amendment and other constitutional safeguards apply only to governmental action — federal, state, or local — or private conduct undertaken at the direction of the government. States, via constitutions or statutes, are free to provide individual protections beyond what is allowed pursuant to the Fourth Amendment.

This report examines the current state of constitutional law on the subject of governmentally mandated drug testing in employment and of students in the public schools, which is followed by a brief review of federal drug-free workplace programs presently in effect.

PERSONAL PRIVACY VS. THE PUBLIC INTEREST

The constitutional focus of governmental drug testing litigation, whether in the employment, public education, or other administrative context, has been the Fourth Amendment, which protects the "right of the people" to be free from "unreasonable searches and seizures" by the government. This constitutional stricture applies to all governmental action, federal, state, and local, by its own force or through the Due Process Clause of the Fourteenth Amendment.[11] Thus, while private actors are not directly affected, the actions of government as an employer are subject to Fourth Amendment scrutiny.[12] Governmental conduct will generally be found to constitute a "search" for Fourth Amendment purposes where it infringes "an expectation of privacy that society is prepared to consider reasonable...."[13] If a search or seizure has occurred, the court must then determine whether the government's action was reasonable under the circumstances.

What a court determines to be "reasonable" depends on the nature of the search and its underlying governmental purpose. Probable cause supported by a warrant is the usual constitutional prerequisite for a criminal search.[14] Even in circumstances where warrantless searches are permitted, they ordinarily "must be based on 'probable cause' to believe that a violation of the law has occurred."[15] Nevertheless, the Supreme Court has determined that neither a warrant nor probable cause is invariably required, and has, under certain circumstances, approved of or let stand "suspicionless" searches, such as sobriety checkpoints,[16] border searches,[17] and metal detector screening.[18]

The Fourth Amendment protects against both civil and criminal investigatory processes, though the need for protection against government intrusion decreases if the investigation is entirely unrelated to criminal law enforcement.[19] In such circumstances, a rule less restrictive on the government, based on "reasonable suspicion" of a civil or regulatory law violation, has become the constitutional norm. However, an exception from even this less demanding standard has been recognized for administrative searches by the government to enforce compliance with a regulatory scheme by persons engaged in a "highly regulated industry" on the theory that the very existence of the regulatory program diminishes reasonable expectations of privacy of those involved in the industry.[20] In such situations, a Fourth Amendment standard based on a balancing test has been crafted by the Court. This "special needs" approach appears to confer optimal power on the government to search where "compelling" reason exists and correspondingly less protection to the individual's "diminished expectation of privacy."

Even prior to *Skinner* and *Von Raab* there was virtual unanimity among the federal courts that governmental drug testing constituted a search that could constitutionally be justified on reasonable suspicion grounds.[21] There is less consensus, however, as to the constitutional propriety of mandatory testing in other circumstances and, particularly, where random testing is imposed as a deterrent to illegal drug use by public employees or for some other governmental objective unrelated to criminal law enforcement. Although not random testing cases, the special needs analysis of *Skinner* and *Von Raab* was subsequently applied by the lower federal courts to justify suspicionless, random testing, provided that the requisite nexus between an employee's duties and public safety or other compelling governmental need was demonstrated.

Workplace Drug Testing and the U.S. Supreme Court

As noted, the U.S. Supreme Court has ruled on Fourth Amendment issues raised by workplace drug testing procedures on several occasions. *Skinner v. Railway Labor Executives Association*[22] upheld post-accident drug and alcohol testing of railway employees involved in major train accidents and incidents, while a program of one-time testing of U.S. Customs employees who apply for promotion to "sensitive jobs" involving carriage of firearms and drug interdiction duties was approved in *National Treasury Employees Union v. Von Raab*.[23] Although *random* testing was not involved, these decisions together establish that "compelling" governmental interests in public safety or national security may, in appropriate circumstances, override the constitutional objections of employees who have a "diminished expectation of privacy" due to the nature of duties they perform or workplace scrutiny to which they are otherwise subjected. *Chandler v. Miller*,[24] on the other hand, voided a Georgia law requiring drug testing of candidates for state office because no "special need" substantial enough to warrant suspicionless searches was shown. Random testing procedures applied to student athletes and participants in extracurricular public school activities have also been approved by the Court. Each of these cases is discussed in-depth below.

In *Skinner*, a panel of the Ninth Circuit had voided on Fourth Amendment grounds Federal Railroad Administration (FRA) regulations requiring breath, blood, and urine tests of railroad workers who are involved in train accidents.[25] The Supreme Court ruled that the entire testing regulation, even portions applicable to certain employee rule infractions that were merely permissive rather than mandatory upon the railroads, carried sufficient government "encouragement, endorsement, and participation ... to implicate the Fourth Amendment."[26] On the merits, the majority held that because "the collection and testing of urine intrudes upon expectations of privacy that society has long recognized as reasonable," FRA testing for drugs and alcohol was a "search" that had to satisfy constitutional standards of reasonableness.[27] The "special needs" of railroad safety, however, made traditional Fourth Amendment requirements of a warrant and probable cause "impracticable" in this context.[28] Nor was "individualized suspicion" deemed by the majority to be a "constitutional floor" where the intrusion on privacy interests are "minimal" and an "important governmental interest" is at stake.[29] According to the Court, covered rail employees had "expectations of privacy" as to their own physical condition that were "diminished by reasons of their participation in an industry that is regulated pervasively to ensure safety...."[30] In these circumstances, the majority held, it was "reasonable" to conduct the tests, even in the absence of a warrant or reasonable suspicion that any employee may be impaired.[31]

The Court also rejected another line of attack against the challenged tests which proceeds from the generally accepted scientific and judicial view that standard test protocols are capable indicators only of prior drug use but are not a measure of current job impairment or drug influence. Because of this fact, a number of lower federal courts had voided certain drug tests for not being reasonably related to legitimate governmental interests in assuring employee fitness or competence.[32] In *Skinner*, however, the majority found the information provided by the tests to be a valid investigative tool which "may allow the FRA to reach an informed judgment as to how a particular accident occurred."[33] In addition, the government "may take all necessary and reasonable regulatory steps to prevent and deter" forbidden drug use by the covered employees.[34]

In the *Von Raab* case, handed down on the same day as *Skinner*, the Supreme Court upheld drug testing of U.S. Customs Service personnel who sought transfer to certain "sensitive" positions, namely those involving drug interdiction, carrying firearms, or access to classified information, without a requirement of reasonable individualized suspicion. The testing procedure was administered once the employee sought transfer to the sensitive position upon five days notice by the Customs Service. Thus, the drug test in *Von Raab* was conditioned on the employee's own action in seeking a transfer and no adverse consequence flowed from a later withdrawn transfer application.[35] According to the Court:

> the Government's compelling interests in preventing the promotion of drug users to positions where they might endanger the integrity of our Nation's borders or the life of the citizenry outweigh the privacy interests of those who seek promotions to those positions, who enjoy a diminished expectation of privacy by virtue of the special physical and ethical demands of those positions.[36]

Neither the absence of "any perceived drug problem among Customs employees," nor the possibility that "drug users can avoid detection with ease by temporary abstinence," would defeat the program because "the possible harm against which the Government seeks to guard is substantial [and] the need to prevent its occurrence furnishes an ample justification for reasonable searches calculated to advance the Government's goal."[37]

The Court's rulings in *Skinner* and *Von Raab* established several constitutional standards potentially relevant to the random testing issue. First, reasonable suspicion was not a constitutional threshold for all governmental drug testing and, therefore, may not preclude carefully crafted random testing in the public sector. Equally important, the balancing test in those cases, based on the "special needs" of the government for assuring transportation safety and the integrity of the federal drug interdiction effort, may as readily be transposed to other regulatory environments where public employees — or, perhaps, applicants for other governmental benefits — may enjoy a "diminished expectation of privacy." Third, as noted above, the Court rejected earlier decisions that had faulted drug testing methodologies due to their inability to detect *present* drug impairment as opposed to simple *past* drug use. Beyond *detection*, it appears the government may have a legitimate interest in *deterring* employee drug use and that drug test evidence may be relevant to "compelling" governmental concerns.

Conversely, the Court, in *Chandler v. Miller*,[38] disapproved a 1990 Georgia statute requiring candidates for Governor, Lieutenant Governor, Attorney General, the state judiciary and legislature, and certain other elective offices, to file a certification that they have tested negatively for illegal drug use. The majority opinion noted several factors distinguishing the Georgia law from drug testing requirements upheld in earlier cases. First, there was no "fear or suspicion" of generalized illicit drug usage by state elected officials in the law's background that might pose a "concrete danger demanding departure from the Fourth Amendment's main rule."[39] The Court noted that while not an invariable constitutional prerequisite, evidence of historical drug abuse by the group targeted for testing might "shore up an assertion of special need for a suspicionless general search program."[40] Secondly, the law did not serve as a "credible means" to detect or deter drug abuse by public officials. Since the timing of the test was largely controlled by the candidate rather than the state, legal compliance could be achieved by mere temporary abstinence.[41] A final "telling difference" between the Georgia case and earlier rulings stemmed from the "relentless scrutiny" to which candidates for public office are subjected, as compared to persons working in less exposed work environments. Any drug abuse by public officials is far more likely to be detected in the ordinary course of events, making suspicionless testing less necessary than in the case of safety-sensitive positions beyond the public view.[42]

EMPLOYEE DRUG TESTING AFTER *SKINNER* AND *VON RAAB*

Federal courts in the wake of *Skinner* and *Von Raab* have generally approved random or other periodic testing of public employees, or workers in heavily regulated industries, provided that the specific jobs covered are directly related to "compelling" public safety, national security, or drug interdiction functions of the government, and testing is undertaken pursuant to a plan that avoids arbitrary application.[43] A generalized desire for workplace "integrity," absent a heightened governmental interest, has usually been found insufficient to warrant random or other routine testing of governmental employees in the absence of individualized suspicion.

Most courts have resisted suspicionless testing procedures as applied to administrative or office personnel who do not pose a threat to public safety or national security. Among programs that have been voided for "overbreadth" are a plan by the Justice Department to test all criminal prosecutors and employees with access to grand jury proceedings;[44] post-accident testing of Office of Personnel Management employees who drive motor vehicles;[45] U.S. Coast Guard drug testing regulations requiring random screening of all private employees aboard commercial vessels;[46] and post-accident testing of any teacher, aide, or clerical workers injured on the job.[47]

What emerges is a pattern of case-by-case judicial decisionmaking as to the "reasonableness" of testing in the circumstances presented. Consequently, broad-based testing programs that fail to account for distinctions among employees in terms of the public safety or national security sensitivity of their duties are less likely to pass constitutional scrutiny.

National Security

Courts have upheld random testing programs that were designed to protect sensitive information. In the Justice Department case, *Harmon v. Thornburgh*,[48] the U.S. Court of Appeals for the District of Columbia ruled that protection of sensitive information — one of the governmental interests cited in *Von Raab* — justified the Department's need to test employees with top secret clearances, but not all federal employees involved in grand jury proceedings. The court elaborated:

> Whatever "truly sensitive" information includes, we agree that it encompasses top secret national security information....We do not believe, however, that the government's interest in preserving all its secrets can justify the testing of all federal prosecutors or of all employees with access to grand jury proceedings. We recognize that every employee within the three categories will have access to information which he is duty-bound not to divulge. But whatever the precise contours of "truly sensitive" information intended by the *Von Raab* Court, we believe that the term cannot include *all* information which is confidential or closed to public view. A very wide range of government employees — including clerks, typists, or messengers — will potentially have access to information of this sort.[49]

The U.S. Court of Appeals for the D.C. Circuit also upheld a random drug testing policy for certain White House employees.[50] In a unanimous decision, the appellate panel found that the employees' rights to be free from random drug testing was outweighed not only by the government's need to protect the President, but also by the government's need to assure the public that it is protecting the President. "The public interest the government is seeking to protect is undoubtedly of the utmost importance. Few events debilitate the nation more than the assassination of the President."[51] The court noted the link between the risk posed by a drug-using OEOB permanent passholder and the potential harm to the President or the Vice President was "direct" and "immediate."[52] It likened the situation to that of an employee with access to top-secret information, where "a single incident could be disastrous." To highlight this direct connection, the opinion observes:

> It is possible that a drug-using OEOB passholder could be blackmailed into using his access to the building to assist in an attack on the President. Given the importance of protecting the President's safety, this is all that is required to make this particular search reasonable. It therefore does not violate the Fourth Amendment.[53]

Public Safety

The government's "compelling" interest in public safety may also justify suspicionless random testing in certain circumstances. For example, after *Von Raab*, the Customs Service drug testing program was expanded from frontline drug interdiction personnel to cover random testing of employees in traditional office environments who had access to databases targeting contraband shipments and inspections. In *National Treasury Employees Union v. U.S. Customs Service*,[54] the D.C. Circuit noted that, because of its link to drug smuggling, the government had an "obvious and compelling" interest in preserving the confidentiality of this database that outweighed the privacy expectations of employees, particularly in light of the intense background checks they underwent prior to employment.[55] Similarly, random testing has been permitted of workers in the transportation,[56] hospital,[57] nuclear power and civilian chemical weapons industries,[58] and of all federal correctional officers of the Bureau of Prisons[59] due to the gravity of risk to be averted by the governmental program.

However, several lower courts have invalidated certain drug testing programs because they "cast too wide a net" in defining categories of persons who must be subjected to random testing procedures. *National Federation of*

Federal Employees (NFFE) v. Cheney[60] considered a program that tested civilian employees in the Department of the Army.[61] The random testing of 2,800 civilian employees who flew and serviced Army aircraft and 3,700 civilian law enforcement personnel at Army facilities was upheld, as well as testing of "direct service" employees, mainly drug counselors, in the Army's alcohol and drug abuse prevention program. But, the court rejected a program of random testing for those employees that "work in a more traditional office environment" simply because they were in the "chain of custody" of urine samples.[62]

In *American Federation of Federal Employees v. Sullivan,*[63] the court had to determine whether it was constitutional to randomly drug test motor vehicle operators who did not carry passengers. As dictated by *Skinner* and *Von Raab*, the court balanced the government's interest in conducting the tests against the individual's privacy expectations. The court observed:

> The government's interest here is the safety risk that an impaired government driver might pose to other drivers on the road. While not insubstantial, this is obviously no different than the interest the public and the government have in keeping potentially impaired driver off the road. If there is a sufficient "special governmental need" to permit warrantless searches..., then the federal government could proceed to test any and all drivers on the road.[64]

Because the federal agency employees did not carry passengers and did not have access to classified information, the court found that neither the passenger safety rationale nor national security concerns were applicable. For these reasons, the court held that it would be unconstitutional to subject these motor vehicle operators to random drug tests.[65]

State or local mandatory testing programs for police or correctional personnel, firefighters, and other "public safety" personnel have usually met with at least qualified judicial approval. In *Guiney v. Roach,*[66] the First Circuit upheld random testing of Boston police officers who were involved in drug interdiction or who carried firearms, but remanded the case for further consideration regarding random testing of other officers. Similarly, the Sixth Circuit has upheld mandatory testing of firefighters and police officers, concluding that there is no requirement of individualized suspicion when testing employees whose duties are "fraught with ... risks of injury to others...."[67]

The Seventh Circuit in *Taylor v. O 'Grady*[68] held that the Cook County Department of Corrections could constitutionally require employees who "(1) [] had regular access to inmate population, (2) [] reasonable opportunity to smuggle drugs into the inmate population, [or] (3) [] access to firearms" to submit to annual drug testing without advanced warning as to the specific timing of the testing. The program was unconstitutional as applied to other personnel "[s]ince those officers with only administrative or clerical duties or otherwise lacking contact with the jail population do not threaten claimed dangers if impaired while on duty, and since the record does not show they are able to smuggle drugs to the prisoners, the Department gains nothing by testing them."[69] Random or other periodic testing of police and other public safety officers also has been approved by many state courts to confront the issue.

The Fifth Circuit's decision, *Aubrey v. School Board of Lafayette Parish*,[70] emphasizes the need to not only avoid overly broad testing coverage, but also to include certain procedural safeguards in implementing such a policy in accordance with the Fourth Amendment. The question before the court was whether an elementary school custodian was a "safety-sensitive" position that could be randomly tested for illegal drug usage. The district court had approved the testing, arguing the custodian was in a safety-sensitive position because he "handles poisonous solvents and lawn mowers, things that could be dangerous to small children if not handled in a safety-conscious manner."[71] In reversing, the appellate court noted that intrusions on personal privacy that may be unreasonable in some contexts "may be rendered entirely reasonable by the operational realities of the workplace."[72] Valid and compelling public interests must be weighed against the interference with individual liberty. This meant that mandatory testing had to be limited to sensitive positions and hedged with procedural safeguards, such as giving notice to individuals that they may be randomly tested. In this case, however:

> [n]o evidence was presented to show which positions are considered safety sensitive and which are not, or whether the policy at the elementary school would differ from that at a high school. Nor was any evidence presented to show whether employees in safety-sensitive positions had notice that they would be subject to random drug testing, or what kind of notice they received, or even if [the custodian] had received notice.[73]

Preemployment Drug Testing

Based on the rationale that applicants for employment do not have the same expectations of privacy as current employees, the courts have often permitted preemployment testing as a condition of public employment. The *Von Raab* case itself presented preemployment issues in that the testing there was required as part of the application process for drug enforcement duty. Federal appellate decisions since have generally approved preemployment and probationary testing rules for public employees or workers in federally regulated industries, especially for safety- sensitive positions.[74]

However, lower courts often have rejected more broadly-based applicant screening programs. For example, a federal district court in *Georgia Association of Educators v. Harris*[75] enjoined preemployment testing of all applicants for state jobs in the State of Georgia because it defied the special needs approach of *Skinner* and *Von Raab*, stating:

> The court finds it difficult to even begin applying that balancing test, however, because defendants have failed to specifically identify any governmental interest that is sufficiently compelling to justify testing *all* job applicants. Moreover, defendants remain oblivious to *Von Raab's* (and indeed, the fourth amendment's [*sic*]) requirement that it connect its interest in testing to the particular job duties of the applicants it wishes to test. Instead, defendants attempt to justify their comprehensive drug testing program based on a generalized governmental interest in maintaining a drug-free workplace. Defendants' position is untenable because neither *Von Raab* nor its progeny recognize such a generalized interest as sufficiently compelling to outweigh an individual's fourth amendment rights.[76]

Student Drug Testing in the Public Schools

Courts have interpreted the Fourth Amendment as providing more leeway to test students for drugs in the school setting, as compared to testing adults in the public employment context. In *Veronia School District 47J v. Acton*,[77] the High Court first considered the constitutionality of student drug testing in the public schools. At issue there was a school district program for random drug testing of high school student athletes, which had been implemented in response to a perceived increase in student drug activity. All student athletes and their parents had to sign forms consenting to testing, which occurred at the season's beginning and randomly thereafter on a weekly basis for the season's duration. Students who tested positive were given the option of either participating in a drug assistance program or being suspended from athletics for the current and following season.[78]

A 6 to 3 majority of the Court upheld the program against Fourth Amendment challenge. Central to the majority's rationale was the "custodial and tutelary" relationship that is created when children are "committed to the temporary custody of the State as school master," in effect "permitting a degree of supervision and control that could not be exercised over free adults."[79] Students had diminished expectations of privacy by virtue of routinely required medical examinations, a factor compounded in the case of student athletes by insurance requirements, minimum academic standards, and the "communal undress" and general lack of privacy in the sports' locker rooms. Because "school sports are not for the bashful," student athletes were found to have a lower expectation of privacy than other students.[80]

Balanced against this diminished privacy interest was the nature of the intrusion and importance of the governmental interest at stake. First, the school district had mitigated actual intrusion by implementing urine collection procedures that simulated conditions "nearly identical to those typically encountered in public restrooms," by analyzing the urine sample only for presence of illegal drugs — not for other medical information, such as the prevalence of disease or pregnancy, and by insuring that positive test results were not provided to law enforcement officials.[81]

School officials unquestionably had an interest in deterring student drug use as part of their "special responsibility of care and direction" toward students.[82] That interest was magnified in *Veronia* by judicial findings that, prior to implementation of the program, "a large segment of the student body, particularly those involved in interscholastic athletics, was in a state of rebellion ... fueled by drug and alcohol abuse...."[83] Consequently, the Court approved the school district's drug testing policy reasoning that the Fourth Amendment only requires that government officials adopt reasonable policies, not the least intrusive ones available. The majority in *Veronia*, however, cautioned "against the assumption that suspicionless drug-testing will readily pass muster in other constitutional contexts."[84]

A division of opinion soon emerged among the lower courts as to how broadly *Veronia* could be applied to permit "suspicionless" drug testing that included student groups beyond athletes and in cases where there was no evidence of a systemic drug problem among the student body. For example, the Seventh and Eighth Circuits in nearly identical cases, *Todd v. Rush County*

Schools[85] and *Miller v. Wilkes*,[86] respectively upheld random drug testing policies that applied not only to student athletes, but also to students participating in any other extracurricular activity, without an identifiable drug problem among the affected student populations in either case.

Parting company with the *Todd* line of decisions was *Trinadad School District No. 1 v. Lopez*,[87] where the Colorado Supreme Court disapproved of a policy for drug testing all students in extracurricular activities where there was no convincing evidence of higher drug usage rates by students participating in extracurricular activities, or that the reasonable privacy expectations of such students had been so diminished by constraints of the sports culture, or otherwise, as those imposed on student athletes in *Veronia.*

This conflict among the circuits was ultimately settled by the Supreme Court in a 2002 decision, *Board of Education of Independent School District No. 92 of Pottawatomie County v. Earls.*[88] In 1998 the Tecumseh Public School District adopted a policy that required "suspicionless drug testing" of students wishing to participate "in any extracurricular activity." Such activities included Future Farmers of America, Future Homemakers of America, academic teams, band, chorus, cheerleading, and athletics. Any student who refused to submit to random testing for illegal drugs was barred from all such activities, but was not otherwise subject to penalty or academic sanction. Lindsay Earls challenged the district's policy "as a condition" to her membership in the high school's show choir, marching band, and academic team, but did not protest the policy as applied to student athletics.

By a 5 to 4 vote, the U.S. Supreme Court held that the Tecumseh school district's random drug testing program was a "reasonable means" of preventing and deterring student drug use and did not violate the Fourth Amendment. In its role as "guardian and tutor," the majority reasoned, the state has responsibility for the discipline, health, and safety of students whose privacy interests are correspondingly limited and subject to "greater control than those for adults."[89] Moreover, students who participate in extracurricular activities "have a limited expectation of privacy" as they participate in the activities and clubs on a voluntary basis, subject themselves to other intrusions of privacy, and meet official rules for participation.[90] The fact that student athletes in the *Veronia* case were regularly subjected to physical exams and communal undress was not deemed "essential" to the outcome there. Instead, that decision "depended primarily upon the school's custodial responsibility and authority," which was equally applicable to athletic and nonathletic activities.[91]

The testing procedure itself, involving collection of urine samples, chain of custody, and confidentiality of results, was found to be "minimally intrusive" and "virtually identical" to that approved by the Court in *Veronia*. In particular, the opinion notes test results were kept in separate confidential files only available to school employees with a "need to know," were not disclosed to law enforcement authorities, and carried no disciplinary or academic consequences other than limiting extracurricular participation. "Given the minimally intrusive nature of the sample collection and the limited uses to which the test results are put, we conclude that the invasion of student's privacy is not significant."[92]

The majority concluded that neither "individualized suspicion" nor a "demonstrated problem of drug abuse" were necessary predicates for a student drug testing program, and there is no "threshold level" of drug use that need be satisfied.[93] "Finally, we find that testing students who participate in extracurricular activities is a reasonably effective means of addressing the School District's legitimate concerns in preventing, deterring, and detecting drug use."[94]

SUSPICIONLESS DRUG TESTING IN OTHER REGULATORY CONTEXTS

While the focus of judicial scrutiny has largely remained fixed on workplace and public school drug testing, questions have also arisen in regard to testing in other administrative venues. A growing body of case law has developed from the efforts of lower federal and state courts to apply the "special needs" approach to an expanding array of governmental programs and regulatory activities. The Third Circuit, for example, anticipated *Skinner* and *Von Raab* when it upheld mandatory testing of horse racing jockeys, officials, and trainers in *Shoemaker v. Handel*,[95] a decision which has since been extended to other participants in that "heavily regulated" industry.[96]

In another regulatory context, the Illinois Supreme Court in *Fink v. Ryan*[97] upheld that state's "implied consent" statute under the "special needs" exception to the Fourth Amendment and its state constitutional counterpart. The Illinois law authorizes chemical testing for drugs or alcohol of drivers who are arrested and issued a traffic citation for any accident causing serious injury or death. No individualized suspicion was required because the state's special need to suspend and deter chemically impaired drivers went beyond normal law enforcement. Moreover, drivers' expectation of privacy was "diminished" by the highly regulated character of automobile usage upon state highways and because state law imposes a separate duty on drivers in such circumstances to remain at the scene to assist injured parties and law enforcement officials.[98]

On the other hand, the Court has struck down drug testing policies that primarily serve criminal law enforcement purposes. In *Ferguson v. City of Charleston*,[99] the Supreme Court invalidated a drug testing policy of pregnant women, specifically rejecting the state's invocation of the special needs doctrine. In response to the problem of cocaine abuse by expectant mothers and its deleterious impact on fetuses, the City of Charleston joined with a state university hospital to develop a plan to test certain pregnant women for illegal drug abuse. Women who tested positively for drugs during pregnancy were provided substance abuse treatment. If these women tested positive a second time or missed a treatment session, they were arrested. Women who tested positive after labor were reported to police and arrested immediately.[100] Women arrested under the policy complained that the warrantless and unconsented drug tests were conducted for criminal investigatory purposes and were therefore unconstitutional.[101]

The Court deemed the balancing test of *Von Raab*, *Veronia*, and *Chandler* inappropriate to the case at hand because the "central and indispensable feature of the policy from its inception was the use of law enforcement to coerce patients into substance abuse treatment."[102] A special need may justify suspicionless drug testing under a program devised for a "proper governmental purpose other than law enforcement."[103] But the exception to Fourth Amendment warrant requirements did not apply "given the pervasive involvement of law enforcement with the development and application of the [drug testing] policy."[104]

Federally Mandated Workplace Drug Testing Programs

The Federal Government by statute or executive order has adopted drug-free workplace requirements applicable to federal executive branch agencies, employment in various federally regulated industries, federal contractors and recipients of federal financial assistance. E.O. 12564, issued on September 15, 1986, requires programs to be established by each department or agency within the executive branch to test for illegal drug use by federal employees in sensitive positions and for voluntary employee drug testing.[105] A "sensitive" position is one that an agency head declares "Special Sensitive," "Critical Sensitive," or "Noncritical-Sensitive" pursuant to the Federal Personnel Manual or sensitive under E.O. 10450. It also includes

> an employee who has been ... or may be granted access to classified information, individuals serving under Presidential appointments, law enforcement officers..., and [o]ther positions that the agency head determines involve law enforcement, national security, the protection of life and property, public health or safety, or other functions requiring a high degree of trust or confidence.

In addition, an executive branch employee may be tested based on "reasonable suspicion" of illegal drug use, during an authorized investigation of an accident or unsafe practice, or to follow-up counseling or rehabilitation for illegal drug use through an employee assistance program. Applicants for employment may also be tested.[106] Technical standards to govern specimen collection, scientific analysis, laboratory certification, medical review of positive test results, and access to records are set forth in guidelines issued by the Department of Health and Human Services.[107]

Private employers obtaining federal contracts or grants must also take specified steps to maintain a drug-free workplace. The Drug-Free Workplace Act of 1988[108] covers all entities receiving contract awards of $100,000 or more, all contracts awarded to individuals, and all recipients of federal grants, regardless of grant amount. Specifically, contractors and grantees must certify to the contracting or grantmaking agency that they "will provide a drug-free workplace by publishing a statement prohibiting unlawful manufacture, distribution, dispensation, possession, or use of a controlled substance" in the workplace, "and specifying the actions that will be taken against [offending] employees."[109] The statute also mandates that employees be told about the potential perils of workplace drug abuse and of "available drug counseling, rehabilitation, and employee assistance programs." As a condition of employment, workers are required to report any criminal conviction for drug-related activity in the workplace, and the employer, in turn, must notify the contracting or granting agency and impose appropriate sanctions upon convicted employees. Federal contracts or grants could be terminated or suspended in cases where the employer fails to make a "good faith effort" to maintain a drug-free workplace.[110] The act, however, does not mandate testing employees for illegal drug use.[111]

The Drug-Free Workplace Act of 1998[112] is the small business counterpart to the 1988 Act described above. The 1998 Act establishes financial incentives to encourage development of drug-free workplace programs by small business employers. Under this law, certain eligible businesses may receive financial assistance from the Small Business Administration (SBA) to implement a drug-free workplace program that meets the standards outlined in the act. Such a program may include employee drug testing.[113]

Some statutes and regulations have been enacted that impose drug testing requirements beyond those mandated by the 1988 Drug-Free Workplace Act. For example, the Department of Defense (DOD) implemented special drug testing requirements for certain DOD contractors via the Federal Acquisition Regulations Supplement.[114] All contracts involving "access to classified information," and any other domestic contract the agency's "contracting officer determines ... necessary for reasons of national security or for the purpose of protecting health or safety" must include a provision obligating the contractor to establish a drug testing program for employees in "sensitive positions" as part of the contractor's duty to maintain a drug- free workplace.[115]

The Civil Space Employee Testing Act of 1991[116] requires the establishment of a program to test for use of alcohol and controlled substances by employees and contractors of the National Aeronautics and Space Administration (NASA) whose duties include "responsibility for safety-sensitive, security, or national security functions." These testing programs must provide for preemployment, reasonable suspicion, random, and post-accident testing, and they also may include periodic recurring testing if warranted. Furthermore, the testing procedures must incorporate the Department of Health and Human Services (DHHS) mandatory testing and record keeping procedures applicable to federal workplace drug testing programs under E.O. 12564.

Mandatory drug and alcohol testing regulations also apply to transportation workers whose jobs have safety and security implications. The Omnibus Transportation Employee Testing Act of 1991[117] requires substance abuse testing, both for alcohol and unlawful drugs, by numerous employers under the jurisdiction of the Department of Transportation (DOT), which include but are not limited to the commercial trucking, railway, aviation, and mass transit industries. Each DOT operating agency maintains its own list of positions considered safety-sensitive. Five types of drug testing are authorized by the act: preemployment, reasonable suspicion, random, post-accident, and periodic recurring. Employees who test positive for drug or alcohol use may be subject to disqualification or dismissal from employment. As part of their substance abuse testing program, employers must also establish drug rehabilitation programs for their employees.[118]

Conclusion

Constitutional law on the subject of governmentally mandated drug testing is primarily an outgrowth of the Fourth Amendment prohibition on unreasonable searches and seizures. Judicial exceptions to traditional requirements of a warrant and individualized suspicion for "administrative" searches have been extended to random drug testing of public employees and school students where the government is able to demonstrate a "special need" beyond the demands of ordinary law enforcement.

In the public employment setting, however, special needs analysis has largely been confined to relatively narrow circumstances directly implicating "compelling" public safety, law enforcement, or national security interests of the government. More generalized governmental concerns for the "integrity" or efficient operation of the public workplace have usually not been deemed sufficient to justify interference with the "reasonable expectation of privacy" of workers or other individuals to be tested. Additionally, warrantless, suspicionless drug testing programs that serve primarily a criminal law enforcement purpose are likely to be unconstitutional.

The constitutional parameters of "special needs" analysis is outlined in a series of Supreme Court rulings. In *Skinner v. Railway Labor Executives Association*, the U.S. Supreme Court upheld post-accident drug and alcohol testing of railway employees after major train accidents or incidents, and it approved the testing of U.S. Customs employees seeking promotion to certain "sensitive" jobs involving firearms use, drug interdiction duties, or access to classified information in *National Treasury Employees Union v. Von Raab*. These decisions established that "compelling" governmental interests in public safety or national security may, in appropriate circumstances, override constitutional objections to testing procedures by employees whose privacy expectations are diminished by the nature of their duties or workplace scrutiny to which they are otherwise subject. In *Veronia School District v. Acton,* the Supreme Court first approved of random drug testing procedures for high school student athletes, a holding that was subsequently extended, in *Board of Education of Independent School District No. 92 of Pottawatomie County v.*

Earls, to permit random drug testing of students participating in non-athletic extracurricular activities. However, the Court placed limitations on the "special needs" doctrine when, in *Chandler v. Miller*, it voided a Georgia law requiring drug testing of candidates for state office for lack of a governmental need substantial enough to warrant suspicionless searches. Additionally, the Court generally has struck down drug testing policies that primarily serve criminal law enforcement purposes, such as in *Ferguson v. City of Charleston*.

End Notes

[1] 489 U.S. 602 (1989).

[2] 489 U.S. 656 (1989).

[3] 515 U.S. 646 (1995).

[4] Policemen's Benevolent Assoc. v. Township of Washington, 850 F.2d 133 (1989).

[5] United Transportation Union v. Southeastern Pennsylvania Transportation Authority (SEPTA), 863 F.2d 1110 (3d Cir.), cert. denied, 109 S.Ct. 3209 (1989) (approved random urinalysis testing of around 2,600 transit "operating engineers" in "safety sensitive" positions over a one-year period, and breathalyzer tests for close to 5,400 such workers annually).

[6] Alverado v. Washington Public Power Supply Systems and Bechtel Construction, Inc., 111 Wash.2d 424 (Wash. 1988), cert. denied, 490 U.S. 1004 (1989).

[7] Bell v. Thornburgh, 878 F.2d 484 (D.C. Cir. 1989), cert. denied 493 U.S. 1056 (1990).

[8] National Federation of Federal Employees v. Cheney, 884 F.2d 603 (D.C. Cir. 1989), cert. denied, 496 U.S. 936 (1990).

[9] Board of Education of Independent School District No. 92 of Pottawatomie County v. Earls, 536 U.S. 822 (2002).

[10] 520 U.S. 305 (1997).

[11] Mapp v. Ohio, 367 U.S. 643, 655 (1961).

[12] O'Connor v. Ortega, 480 U.S. 709, 715 (1987).

[13] United States v. Jacobsen, 466 U.S. 109, 113 (1984).

[14] Camara v. Municipal Court, 387 U.S. 523, 528-29 (1967) ("one governing principle, justified by history and by current experience, has consistently been followed: except in certain carefully defined classes of cases, a search of private property without proper consent is 'unreasonable' unless it has been authorized by a valid search warrant.").

[15] New Jersey v. T.L.O., 469 U.S. 325, 340 (1985).

[16] Michigan Dep't of State Police v. Sitz, 496 U.S. 444 (1990).

[17] United States v. Martinez-Fuerte, 428 U.S. 543 (1976) (upholding suspicionless searches that occur at fixed checkpoints near the border).

[18] See, e.g., United States v. Vigil, 989 F.2d 337, 339 (9th Cir. 1993).

[19] South Dakota v. Opperman, 428 U.S. 364, n.5 (1976) ("The probable-cause approach is unhelpful when analysis centers upon the reasonableness of routine, administrative caretaking functions [such as inventory searches], particularly when no claim is made that the protective procedures are a subterfuge for criminal investigations."); Wyman v. James, 400 U.S. 309, 322-325 (1971) (Visits by government officials to the homes of welfare recipients for the purpose of evaluating their eligibility for benefits do not abridge the Fourth Amendment.).

[20] Donovan v. Dewey, 452 U.S. 594, 600 (1981).

[21] "Reasonable suspicion is a lesser standard than probable cause. There is a reasonable suspicion when there is some articulable basis for suspecting that the employee is using illegal drugs.

Put another way, there is reasonable suspicion when there is some quantum of individualized suspicion as opposed to an inarticulate hunch. Reasonable suspicion may be based on statements made by other employees and tips from informants. Even probable cause can be based on informants' tips when the totality of the circumstances indicates a fair probability of accuracy." Smith v. White, 666 F. Supp. 1085, 1089-90 (E.D.Tenn. 1987) (internal citations omitted).

22 489 U.S. 602 (1989).

23 489 U.S. 656 (1989).

24 520 U.S.305 (1997).

25 *Skinner*, 489 U.S. at 606.

26 *Id.* at 615-16.

27 *Id.* at 617.

28 *Id.* at 631.

29 *Id.* at 624.

30 *Id.* at 627.

31 *Id.* at 633.

32 E.g., Jones v. McKenzie, 833 F.2d 335, 340 (D.C.Cir. 1987); Ry. Labor Executive Ass'n v. Burnley, 839 F.2d 1507 (9th Cir. 1988); Harmon v. Meese, 690 F. Supp. 65 (D.D.C. 1988).

33 *Skinner*, 489 U.S. at 632.

34 *Id.* at 632-33.

35 *Id.* at 630-33.

36 *Von Raab*, 489 U.S. at 679.

37 *Id.* at 673-75.

38 Chandler v. Miller, 520 U.S. 305 (1997).

39 *Id.* at 318-19.

40 *Id.* at 319.

41 *Id.* at 39-20.

42 *Id.* at 321.

43 Ford v. Dowd, 931 F.2d 1286 (8th Cir. 1991) (invalidating drug testing of individual police officer in absence of specific plan, whether applied randomly or routinely, and in absence of reasonable suspicion of drug use); Jackson v. Gates, 975 F.2d 648 (9th Cir. 1992) (invalidating drug testing of individual police officer in absence of random testing scheme and in absence or articulable basis for suspecting drug use).

44 Harmon v. Thornburgh, 878 F.2d 484 (D.C. Cir. 1989).

45 Connelly v. Newman, 753 F. Supp. 293, 297 (N.D. Cal. 1990) (absence of "sufficient threat to public safety" undermined governmental interest in testing OPM drivers).

46 Transp. Inst. v. U.S. Coast Guard, 727 F.Supp. 648, 657 (D.D.C.1990) (striking down "broadly drawn" federal requirement that all private workers on private commercial ships be randomly tested because the "immediacy or gravity of the potential safety threat [not] sufficient" to justify the policy.).

47 United Teachers of New Orleans v. Orleans Parish Sch. Bd., 142 F.3d 853 (5th Cir. 1998) (striking down policy that required testing without "any suggestion that a triggering injury was caused by any misstep of the employee to be tested."). But see, Knox County Educ. Ass'n v. Knox County Bd. of Educ., 158 F.3d 361 (6th Cir. 1999) (upholding suspicionless testing of public school teachers upon appointment or transfer).

48 Harmon v. Thornburgh, 878 F.2d 484 (D.C. Cir. 1989).

49 *Id.* at 491-92 (emphasis original). See also, 919 F.2d 170 (D.C.Cir. 1990).

50 110 F.3d 801 (D.C. Cir. 1997).

51 *Id.* at 803-04.

52 *Id.* at 806.

53 *Id.*

[54] 27 F.3d 623 (D.C. Cir. 1994); See also, Nat'l Treasury Employees Union v. Hallet, 756 F. Supp. 947 (E.D.N.Y. 1991) (upholding testing of applicants for Customs Service positions requiring top secret, secret, and confidential security clearances; Nat'l Treasury Employees Union v. Hallet, 776 F. Supp. 680 (E.D.N.Y. 1991) upholding random testing of customs employees directly involved in law enforcement; those with access to or who handle illegal drugs, including chemists and student trainees under their supervision; customs workers who operate forklifts or motor vehicles; and those who carry firearms).

[55] *Nat'l Treasury Employees Union v. U.S. Customs Serv.*, 27 F.3d at 629-30.

[56] United Food & Commercial Workers Int'l Union, Local 558 v. Foster Poultry Farms, 74 F.3d 169 (9th Cir. 1995) (truck drivers); Bluestein v. Skinner, 908 F.2d 451 (9th Cir. 1990) (airline workers); Ry. Labor Executive Ass'n v. Skinner, 934 F.2d 1096 (9th Cir. 1991) (certain railroad employees); Int'l Bhd. of Teamsters v. Dept. of Transp., 932 F.2d 1292 (9th Cir. 1991) (commercial vehicle operators). But see, Rutherford v. City of Albequerque, 77 F.3d 1258 (10th Cir. 1996) (holding the dismissal of city dump truck driver upon return from medical leave based on positive result of unannounced drug test violates the Fourth Amendment).

[57] Kemp v. Claiborne County Hosp., 763 F.Supp. 1362 (S.D.Miss. 1991) (scrub technician in surgery was in safety sensitive position that justified drug testing).

[58] Thomson v. Marsh, 884 F.2d 113 (4th Cir. 1989) (civilian chemical weapons employees).

[59] Am. Fed'n of Gov't Employees v. Roberts, 9 F.3d 1464 (9th Cir. 1993) (upholding random and reasonable suspicion drug testing of all federal correctional officers by theBureau of Prisons).

[60] 884 F.2d 603 (D.C.Cir. 1989).

[61] *Id.* at 615.

[62] *Id.* at 614-15.

[63] 787 F. Supp. 255 (D.D.C. 1992).

[64] *Id.* at 257.

[65] *Id.* See also, Nat'l Treasury Employees Union v. Watkins, 722 F.Supp 766 (D.D.C. 1989) (enjoining the Department of Energy (DOE) from random testing of certain DOE employees in "sensitive positions," including motor vehicle operators and computer specialists involved in security operations, because the court found none of the extraordinary public safety, drug interdiction, and security interests highlighted by *Skinner* and *Von Raab*).

[66] 873 F.2d 1557 (lst Cir. 1989).

[67] Penny v. Kennedy, 915 F.2d 1065, 1067 (6th Cir. 1990).

[68] 888 F.2d 1189 (7th Cir. 1989).

[69] *Id.* at 1197.

[70] 92 F.3d 316 (1996).

[71] *Id.* at 318.

[72] *Id.*

[73] *Id.* at 319.

[74] Willner v. Thornburgh, 928 F.2d 1185 (D.C. Cir. 1991) (approving a testing plan for attorneys applying for positions with the Antitrust Division of the Department of Justice); Int'l Bhd. of Teamsters v. Dept. of Transp., 932 F.2d 1292 (9th Cir. 1991) (approving preemployment testing of truck drivers); O'Connor v. Police Comm'r of Boston, 557 N.E.2d 1146 (1990) (approving random drug testing of police cadets during probationary period); McKensie v. Jackson, 547 N.Y.S.2d 120 (App. Div. 1989) (approving random testing of corrections personnel during one-year probationary employment period); Alverado v. Washington State Pub. Power Supply Sys., 759 P.2d 427 (Wash. 1988) (approving preemployment testing of individuals given access to nuclear power plants).

[75] 749 F. Supp. 1110 (N.D. Ga. 1990).

[76] *Id.* at 1114.

[77] 515 U.S. 646 (1995).

[78] *Id.* at 649-50.
[79] *Id.* at 654-56.
[80] *Id.* at 657.
[81] *Id.* at 658.
[82] *Id.* at 662.
[83] *Id.* at 662-63.
[84] *Id.* at 664-65.
[85] 133 F.3d 984 (7th Cir.1998).
[86] 172 F.3d 574 (8th Cir. 1999).
[87] 963 P.2d 1095 (Colo. 1998).
[88] 536 U.S. 522 (2002).
[89] *Id.* at 830-31.
[90] *Id.* at 831-32.
[91] *Id.* at 831.
[92] *Id.* at 832-34.
[93] *Id.* at 836-37.
[94] *Id.* at 837.
[95] Shoemaker v. Handel, 795 F.2d 1136 (3d Cir. 1986).
[96] See, Carelli v. Ginsburg, 956 F.2d 598 (6th Cir. 1992) (testing of licensed thoroughbred horse trainers); Dimeo v. Griffin, 943 F.2d 679 (7th Cir. 1991) (random searches of jockeys and other horse racing participants); Holtus v. Louisiana State Racing Comm'n, 580 So.2d 469 (La. App. 1991) (random testing of licensees of the state racing commission).
[97] 174 Ill.2d 302 (Ill. 1996).
[98] *Id.* at 310-12.
[99] 532 U.S. 67 (2001).
[100] *Id.* at 71-72.
[101] *Id.* at 73.
[102] *Id.* at 80.
[103] *Id.* at fn. 17.
[104] *Id.* at 85.
[105] 51 Fed. Reg. 32889 (September 17, 1986).
[106] E.O. 12564.
[107] For detailed information on the technical standards, see [http://drugfreeworkplace.gov/FedPgms/Pages/Model_Plan.aspx].
[108] 41 U.S.C. §§701, *et seq.*
[109] 41 U.S.C. §§ 701 and 702.
[110] *Id.*
[111] More detailed information on the Drug-free Workplace Act may be found in implementing rules issued at 54 Fed. Reg. 4946 (January 31, 1989), 54 Fed. Reg. 29908 (June 9, 1994), and 69 Fed. Reg. 19644 (April 13, 2004).
[112] 15 U.S.C. § 654.
[113] *Id.*
[114] Fed. Acquisition Reg. Supp. § 252.223.
[115] Fed. Acquisition Reg. Supp. §§ 252.223-7004 and 223.570-2.
[116] 42 U.S.C. § 2473c.
[117] P.L. 102-143.
[118] For more information on the DOT drug testing program, see 49 C.F.R. Part 40 and [http://www.dot.gov/ost/dapc/].

In: The Fourth Amendment
Editors: Jesse V. Kessler
ISBN: 978-1-61728-885-2

Chapter 7

COMPULSORY DNA COLLECTION: A FOURTH AMENDMENT ANALYSIS

Anna C. Henning

SUMMARY

Relying on different legal standards, courts have historically upheld laws authorizing law enforcement's compulsory collection of deoxyribonucleic acid (DNA) as reasonable under the Fourth Amendment to the U.S. Constitution. However, prior cases reviewed the extraction of DNA samples from people who had been convicted on criminal charges. New state and federal laws authorize the collection of such samples from people who have been arrested or detained but not convicted. On the federal level, the U.S. Department of Justice implemented this expanded authority with a final rule that took effect January 9, 2009.

Only a few courts have reviewed the constitutionality of pre-conviction DNA collection. The two federal district courts to have considered the issue applied the same Fourth Amendment test – the "general balancing" or "general reasonableness" test – but reached opposite conclusions. In *United States v. Pool*, the U.S. District Court for the Eastern District of California held that the government's interest in collecting a DNA sample from a person facing charges outweighed any intrusion of privacy. In *United States v. Mitchell*, the

U.S. District Court for the Western District of Pennsylvania reached the opposite conclusion.

Points of disagreement between the two district court opinions are likely to reemerge as themes in future decisions addressing pre-conviction DNA collection. One difference is whether the defendant's status as a person facing criminal charges was viewed as impacting the scope of Fourth Amendment protection. Another is the extent to which the government was seen as having a legitimate interest in obtaining a DNA sample in particular, rather than a fingerprint or another identifier. Finally, the courts disagreed regarding the degree of the privacy intrusion caused by collecting a DNA sample. The latter questions are framed by a larger debate about the nature and role of DNA in law enforcement. For example, is a DNA sample merely a means by which to identify a person, like a fingerprint? Or does it present a greater privacy intrusion?

A few additional factors might complicate courts' analyses of DNA collection in future cases. For example, emerging scientific research suggests that the type of DNA used in forensic analysis might implicate a greater privacy intrusion than courts had previously assumed. In addition, most courts have yet to review the constitutionality of storing convicts' DNA profiles beyond the time of sentence completion.

INTRODUCTION

In recent years, state and federal laws have facilitated law enforcement's expanded use of deoxyribonucleic acid (DNA) for investigating and prosecuting crimes.[1] Such laws authorize compulsory collection of biological matter, which local law enforcement agencies send to the Federal Bureau of Investigation (FBI) for analysis. The FBI then stores unique DNA profiles in a national distributive database, through which law enforcement officials match individuals to crime scene evidence. Early laws authorized compulsory extraction of DNA only from people convicted for violent or sex-based felonies, such as murder, kidnapping, and offenses "related to sexual abuse" – crimes associated with historically high recidivism rates and for which police were likely to find evidence at crime scenes.[2] Since the turn of the century, new laws have greatly extended the scope of compulsory DNA collection, both by expanding the range of offenses triggering collection authority, and, more recently, by authorizing compulsory collection from people who have been arrested but not convicted.

Litigants have challenged compulsory collection and the subsequent analysis and storage of DNA as unreasonable searches and seizures under the Fourth Amendment to the U.S. Constitution. Although they have reached their conclusions using different analytical approaches, federal and state courts have generally upheld compulsory DNA collection as non-violative of the Fourth Amendment. However, prior cases involved the collection of DNA samples from people who had been convicted of a crime. More recently, a few courts have addressed such collection from arrestees, with differing results. This report examines statutory authorities, constitutional principles, and case law related to compulsory DNA extraction and analyzes potential impacts of recent developments for Fourth Amendment cases.

BACKGROUND ON LAW ENFORCEMENT USE OF DNA

DNA is a complex molecule found in human cells and "composed of two nucleotide strands," which "are arranged differently for every individual except for identical twins."[3] Relatively new technology enables DNA analysts to determine the arrangement of these strands, thereby creating unique DNA profiles.[4]

In the law enforcement context, DNA profiles function like "genetic fingerprints" that aid in matching perpetrators to their crimes.[5] As with fingerprints, law enforcement officers collect DNA samples from specific classes of individuals, such as prisoners. However, compulsory DNA collection generally entails blood or saliva samples rather than finger impressions, and DNA profiles can later match any of many types of biological matter obtained from crime scenes.[6] For these reasons, DNA matching is considered a "critical complement to," rather than merely a supplement for, fingerprint analysis in identifying criminal suspects.[7]

The FBI administers DNA storage and analysis for law enforcement agencies across the country. After a law enforcement agency's phlebotomist collects a blood sample pursuant to state or federal law, the agency submits the sample to the FBI, which creates a DNA profile and stores the profile in the Combined DNA Index System, a database through which law enforcement officers match suspects to DNA profiles at the local, state, and national levels.[8]

FBI analysts create DNA profiles by "decoding sequences of 'junk DNA.'"[9] So-called "junk DNA," the name for "non-genic stretches of DNA not presently recognized as being responsible for trait coding," is "'purposefully selected'" for DNA analysis because it is not "associated with any known physical or medical characteristics," and thus theoretically poses only a minimal invasion of privacy.[10]

STATUTORY FRAMEWORK

The categories of individuals from whom law enforcement officials may require DNA samples has expanded in recent years. The federal government and most states authorize compulsory collection of DNA samples from individuals convicted for specified criminal offenses, including all felonies in most jurisdictions and extending to misdemeanors, such as failure to register as a sex offender or crimes for which a sentence greater than six months applies, in some jurisdictions.[11] In addition, a federal and some state statutes now authorize compulsory collection from people whom the government has arrested or detained but not convicted. As discussed *infra*, the DNA Analysis Backlog Elimination Act 2000, as amended, authorizes compulsory collection from individuals in federal custody, including those detained, arrested, or facing charges, and from individuals on release, parole, or probation in the federal criminal justice system.[12] Under the federal law, if an individual refuses to cooperate, relevant officials "may use or authorize the use of such means as are reasonably necessary to detain, restrain, and collect a DNA sample."[13] State laws vary, but nearly all states authorize compulsory DNA collection from people convicted for specified crimes, and a small but growing number of states also authorize compulsory collection from arrestees.[14]

Expansion of Statutory Authorities for DNA Collection and Analysis

At the federal level, statutory authority for compulsory DNA collection has expanded relatively rapidly. During the 1 990s, a trio of federal laws created the logistical framework for DNA collection, storage, and analysis. The DNA Identification Act of 1994 provided funding to law enforcement agencies for DNA collection and created the FBI's Combined DNA Index

System to facilitate the sharing of DNA information among law enforcement agencies.[15] Next, the Antiterrorism and Effective Death Penalty Act of 1996 authorized grants to states for developing and upgrading DNA collection procedures,[16] and the Crime Identification Technology Act of 1998 authorized additional funding for DNA analysis programs.[17] The resulting framework centers on the Combined DNA Index System; more than 170 law enforcement agencies throughout the country participate in the system. [18]

In recent years, federal and state laws have expanded law enforcement authority for collecting DNA in at least two ways. First, laws have increased the range of offenses which trigger authority for collecting and analyzing DNA. In the federal context, the DNA Analysis Backlog Elimination Act of 2000 limited compulsory extraction of DNA to people who had been convicted of a "qualifying federal offense."[19] Under the original act, "qualifying federal offenses" included limited but selected felonies, such as murder, kidnapping, and sexual exploitation.[20] After September 11, 2001, the USA PATRIOT Act expanded the "qualifying federal offense" definition to include terrorism-related crimes.[21] In 2004, the Justice for All Act further extended the definition to reach all crimes of violence, all sexual abuse crimes, and all felonies.[22] Similarly, almost all states now authorize collection of DNA from people convicted of any felony.[23]

Second, laws have authorized compulsory DNA collection from people who have been detained or arrested but not convicted on criminal charges. The 109th Congress authorized the Attorney General, in his discretion, to require collection from such individuals. Specifically, the DNA Fingerprinting Act of 2005 authorized collection "from individuals who are arrested or from nonU.S. persons who are detained under the authority of the United States."[24] The Adam Walsh Child Protection and Safety Act of 2006 subsequently substituted "arrested, facing charges, or convicted" for the word "arrested" in that authority.[25] The U.S. Department of Justice implemented the authorization in a final rule that took effect January 9, 2009.[26] Mirroring the statutory language, it requires U.S. agencies to collect DNA samples from "individuals who are arrested, facing charges, or convicted, and from non-United States persons who are detained under authority of the United States."[27] As mentioned, some states have likewise enacted laws authorizing collection of arrestees' DNA.[28]

Whereas the increase in the range of triggering offenses appears to be a natural outcome of DNA's success as a forensic tool, the expansion to collection from arrestees appears to be a more legally significant step. Overall, it seems Congress' goal for the expansion to arrestees and those facing charges was to facilitate crime prevention through "the creation of a comprehensive, robust database that will make it possible to catch serial rapists and murderers before they commit more crimes."[29] In background material for its implementing rule, the Justice Department explains that collection from arrestees will facilitate more effective law enforcement for at least two reasons: (1) it will aid in crime prevention by ensuring that the government need not wait until a crime has been committed before creating an individual's DNA profile; and (2) it will allow federal authorities to create DNA profiles for aliens detained in the United States, who might not otherwise undergo judicial proceedings in U.S. courts.[30]

Expungement Provisions

Although Congress expanded statutory authority for DNA collection, it has also provided some protection for arrestees when arrest does not result in conviction. In particular, federal law mandates expungement of DNA samples upon an arrestee's showing of discharge or acquittal.

The FBI and relevant state agencies "shall promptly expunge" DNA information "from the index" upon receipt of "a final court order establishing that such charge has been dismissed or has resulted in an acquittal or that no charge was filed within the applicable time period."[31] Officials must also expunge DNA data for convicts in cases where a conviction is overturned.[32] These provisions apply to DNA collected by state and local law enforcement officers, in addition to DNA collected in the federal justice or detention systems.

FOURTH AMENDMENT OVERVIEW

The Fourth Amendment to the U.S. Constitution provides a right "of the people to be secure in their persons, houses, papers, and effects, against unreasonable searches and seizures."[33] Two fundamental questions arise in every Fourth Amendment challenge. First, does the challenged action constitute a search or seizure by federal or local government and thus trigger the Fourth Amendment right?[34] Second, if so, is the search or seizure "reasonable"?

Search or Seizure

Different tests trigger the Fourth Amendment right depending on whether a litigant challenges government conduct as a seizure or as a search. Seizures involve interference with property rights; a seizure of property occurs when government action "meaningfully interferes" with possessory interests or freedom of movement.[35]

In contrast, searches interfere with personal privacy. Government action constitutes a search when it intrudes upon a person's "reasonable expectation of privacy."[36] A reasonable expectation of privacy requires both that an "individual manifested a subjective expectation of privacy in the searched object" and that "society is willing to recognize that expectation as reasonable."[37]

In general, people have no reasonable expectation of privacy for physical characteristics they "knowingly expos[e] to the public."[38] In evaluating whether people "knowingly expose" identifying characteristics, the Supreme Court has sometimes distinguished the drawing of blood and other internal fluids from the taking of fingerprints. At times, it has signaled that people lack a reasonable expectation of privacy in their fingerprints,[39] but it has held that extraction of blood, urine, and other fluids implicates an intrusion upon a reasonable expectation of privacy, presumably because the former category is "knowingly exposed" to the public while the latter category generally is not.[40]

Under modern Supreme Court precedent, a further complicating factor is that reasonable expectation of privacy depends not only on the type of evidence gathered, but also on the status of the person from whom it is gathered. The inquiry is not simply a yes-or-no determination, but appears to include a continuum of privacy expectations. For example, in *United States v. Knights*, the Court held that the "condition" of probation "significantly diminished" a probationer's reasonable expectation of privacy.[41] This diminished privacy expectation did not completely negate the probationer's Fourth Amendment right; however, it affected the outcome under the Court's Fourth Amendment balancing test.[42]

"Reasonableness" Inquiry When the Fourth Amendment Applies

When government action constitutes a search or seizure, "reasonableness" is the "touchstone" of constitutionality.[43] However, courts apply different standards, in different circumstances, to determine whether searches and seizures are reasonable. The Court's Fourth Amendment analysis falls into three general categories.

The first category involves traditional law enforcement activities, such as arrests or searching of homes. To be reasonable, these activities require "probable cause," which must be formalized by a warrant unless a recognized warrant exception applies.[44] Probable cause is "a fluid concept – turning on the assessment of probabilities in particular factual contexts – not readily, or even usefully, reduced to a neat set of legal rules,"[45] yet it is considered the most stringent Fourth Amendment standard. In the context of issuing warrants, probable cause requires an issuing magistrate to make a "common sense" determination, based on specific evidence, whether there exists a "fair probability" that, for example, an area contains contraband.[46]

The second category, introduced in the Supreme Court case *Terry v. Ohio*, involves situations in which a limited intrusion satisfies Fourth Amendment strictures with a reasonableness standard that is lower than probable cause.[47] For example, in *Terry*, a police officer's patting of the outside of a man's clothing to search for weapons required more than "inchoate and unparticularized suspicion" but was justified by "specific reasonable inferences" that the man might have a weapon.[48] In such situations, courts permit searches justified by "reasonable suspicion," which is a particularized suspicion prompted by somewhat less specific evidence than probable cause requires.[49]

The third category includes "exempted area," "administrative," "special needs," and other "suspicionless" searches. Examples include routine inventory searches, border searches, roadblocks, and drug testing. In these circumstances, courts apply a "general approach to the Fourth Amendment" – also called the "general balancing," "general reasonableness," or "totalityof-the circumstances" test – to determine reasonableness "by assessing, on the one hand, the degree to which [a search or seizure] intrudes upon an individual's privacy and, on the other, the degree to which it is needed for the promotion of legitimate governmental interests."[50] Although the Supreme Court has expanded the scope of application for this test, the approach historically applied only when a search or seizure satisfied parameters for one of several narrow categories. In particular, it applied where a routine, administrative purpose justified regular searches; where a long-recognized exception existed, such as for border searches; or where a "special nee[d], beyond the normal need for law enforcement, [made] the warrant and probable cause requirements impracticable."[51]

In the context of law enforcement's collection of DNA from prisoners, parolees, and others subject to law enforcement supervision, questions remain regarding when a special need, distinct from law enforcement interests, must exist before a court may apply a general reasonableness standard. Although the special needs test arose in the context of drug testing, the Supreme Court has held that probation and other post-conviction punishment regimes qualified as special needs with purposes distinct from law enforcement. For example, in *Griffin v. Wisconsin*, the Court held that a "state's operation of a probation system, like its operation of a school, government office or prison, or its supervision of a regulated industry ... presents 'special needs' beyond law enforcement."[52] As discussed below, later Supreme Court cases seem to suggest that a defendant's post-conviction status, alone, might justify a court's direct application of a general reasonableness test to DNA collection, without any finding of a special need.

Diminishment of Privacy Expectations under Supreme Court Precedent

Since 2000, the Supreme Court has twice applied a general reasonableness test in Fourth Amendment cases involving people serving post-conviction punishments – specifically, in cases involving a probationer and a parolee – without first finding special needs justifying the government action. In both cases, the Court's legal basis for directly applying the general balancing approach was the reduced expectation of privacy to which each defendant was entitled by virtue of his post-conviction status. In addition to providing a justification for rejection of the special needs test, this same diminishment of defendants' privacy expectations also favored the government in the Court's application of the general balancing test.

In *United States v. Knights*, a 2001 case, a California court had sentenced Mark Knights to probation for a drug offense.[53] One condition of his probation was that his "person, property, place of residence," etc., were subject to search "with or without a search warrant."[54] After finding some evidence that appeared to link him with a fire at a local telecommunications vault, a police detective searched Knights' home without a warrant.[55] Emphasizing the curtailment of privacy rights that correspond with probation and other post-conviction punishment regimes, the Court evaluated the search under the general balancing test, without first identifying an administrative purpose or special needs justification.[56] In addition, Knights' diminished expectation of privacy affected the outcome under the Court's general Fourth Amendment balancing test. Noting that "Knights' status as a probationer subject to a search condition informs both sides of that balance," the Court easily upheld the officer's search based on reasonable suspicion.[57]

In *Samson v. California*, a 2006 case, the Court extended *Knight*s to uphold a search of a parolee's pockets, for the first time directly applying the general reasonableness test to a search justified only on the basis of the petitioner's status as a parolee, rather than on any particularized suspicion.[58] As in *Knights*, the *Samson* Court explicitly rejected arguments that a special needs analysis was required; instead, finding that the petitioner's post-conviction status diminished his privacy rights, the Court again directly applied a "general Fourth Amendment approach."[59] In addition, as in *Knights*, the *Samson* court held that a parolee's diminished privacy right affected the outcome of the general balancing test.[60]

It is unclear what other categories of people might be subject to a reduced expectation of privacy by virtue of their status. It appears from Supreme Court dicta that at least a lesser reduction in privacy rights would apply to those in pre-trial detention versus people serving sentences after conviction. In *Knights* and *Samson*, the Supreme Court referred to parolees and probationers as being along a "'continuum' of state-imposed punishments."[61] Furthermore, in *Samson*, the Court held that a parolee lacked "an expectation of privacy that society would recognize as legitimate," because searches were a condition of parole, which was a "'an established variation on imprisonment.'"[62] Lower federal courts have interpreted these and other Supreme Court decisions as suggesting that prisoners' privacy expectations are the most diminished; parolees have the next lowest diminishment in privacy expectations, followed by people on supervised release and probationers.[63] The few U.S. district court cases addressing DNA collection from persons awaiting trial, discussed *infra*, have reached different conclusions regarding the extent to which a person's pre-trial detention diminishes his or her reasonable expectation of privacy.

Case Law on DNA Collection

Courts have uniformly held that compulsory DNA collection and analysis constitutes a search, and thus triggers Fourth Amendment rights.[64] Although some courts have signaled that DNA collection or storage might also constitute a seizure, courts have generally not addressed that question. [65] Thus, the question in cases brought is whether the collection of DNA satisfies the Fourth Amendment reasonableness test.

Reasonableness of Post-Conviction Collection

Prior to the expansion of DNA collection authority to arrestees, nearly all courts that reviewed laws authorizing compulsory DNA collection upheld the laws against Fourth Amendment challenges.[66] Although the U.S. Supreme Court has never accepted a DNA collection case,[67] U.S. Courts of Appeals for the First, Second, Sixth, Seventh, Eight, Ninth, Tenth, and Eleventh Circuits upheld the 2004 version of the federal DNA collection law, which authorized collection and analysis of DNA from people convicted of any felony, certain sexual crimes, and crimes of violence.[68] Likewise, federal courts of appeals have upheld numerous state DNA collection laws.[69]

Courts have relied on different legal tests in these cases.[70] While most courts have directly applied a general reasonableness approach, some courts have first evaluated government actions under the special needs test.[71] The majority of the federal courts of appeals have interpreted *Samson* as affirmatively requiring courts to apply the general reasonableness test, without a special needs prerequisite, at least as applied to prisoners or other individuals with post-conviction status. For example, in *Wilson v. Collins*, the Court of Appeals for the Sixth Circuit interpreted *Samson* as requiring direct application of the general balancing test in a case involving a prisoner.[72] Likewise, in *United States v. Weikert*, a case involving compulsory collection of DNA from a man on supervised release, the Court of Appeals for the First Circuit held that, under *Samson*, a general reasonableness test applied in DNA collections cases.[73]

In contrast, some federal courts of appeals have held that *Samson* did not affect their use of the special needs test in suits challenging DNA collection statutes. For example, the Court of Appeals for the Second Circuit declined to apply *Samson* in *United States v. Amerson*, a case upholding compulsory DNA collection from two individuals on probation, one for larceny and one for wire fraud.[74] The court interpreted *Samson* very narrowly, as applying only in contexts involving a "highly diminished" expectation of privacy.[75] Similarly, although it directly applied the general reasonableness test in *Wilson*, the Sixth Circuit suggested in that case that *Samson* might not apply in a case involving a person who was not a prisoner.[76]

The reading of *Samson* as limited to cases involving a significantly diminished expectation of privacy appears to comport with the Supreme Court's emphasis in *Knights* and *Samson* on the diminished privacy rights that stem from a petitioner's post-conviction status. In *Samson*, the Court framed the question in the case as "whether a condition of release can so diminish or eliminate a released prisoner's reasonable expectation of privacy that a suspicionless search by a law enforcement officer would not offend the Fourth Amendment."[77]

In evaluating post-conviction DNA collection, whether courts apply the special needs test before applying a general reasonableness test in DNA cases has had little or no practical import, because courts have consistently upheld the collection regardless of the standard they apply. Thus, courts have signaled that a change in analytic tools would not affect the ultimate determination of constitutionality in DNA collection cases involving convicted criminals.[78] However, courts addressing collection in the post-conviction context have made clear that their holdings do not apply to collection from arrestees.[79]

Reasonableness as Applied to Arrestees

As mentioned, to date, only a handful of state[80] and federal judicial decisions address compulsory collection of DNA from persons awaiting a criminal trial. Two federal district courts have issued opinions on the issue. In *United States v. Pool*, the U.S. District Court for the Eastern District of California upheld such collection.[81] In *United States v. Mitchell*, the U.S. District Court for the Western District of Pennsylvania reached the opposite result.[82]

In both U.S. district court cases, the government requested a DNA sample after the defendant was arrested pursuant to a criminal indictment but before trial.[83] Both courts applied the general balancing test to determine whether such collection was reasonable under the Fourth Amendment.[84]

Their divergent conclusions can be explained, in part, by the courts' differing characterizations of DNA collection on both sides of the general balancing test. On the privacy intrusion side, the *Pool* court viewed a DNA sample as no more intrusive than fingerprinting.[85] In contrast, the *Mitchell* court noted that DNA has the potential to reveal a host of private genetic information and rejected the analogy to fingerprinting as "pure folly."[86]

The courts' different views of DNA's role also impacted their conclusions on the government interest side of the balancing test. The *Pool* court viewed the government's interest in collecting DNA as equally legitimate as fingerprinting and other identification tools, in which governments have been held to have a sufficient interest.[87] In contrast, because it viewed DNA collection as presenting a far greater privacy intrusion than fingerprinting, the *Mitchell* court held that although the government has a legitimate interest in identifying suspects, that interest is one "that can be satisfied with a fingerprint and photograph" rather than with the more intrusive DNA sample.[88]

Another explanation for the different outcomes is the courts' different views of the implication of an indictment for a defendant's reasonable expectation of privacy. The *Pool* court viewed a grand jury's finding of probable cause at an indictment as a "watershed event," pursuant to which it is constitutional to detain a defendant or otherwise restrict a defendant's liberty.[89] Thus, the *Pool* court found that a post-indictment arrestee has a substantially diminished reasonable expectation of privacy. However, it expressly limited its holding to cases in which DNA collection occurs after an indictment.[90]

Criticizing the *Pool* opinion, the *Mitchell* court stated that it is "loath to elevate a finding of probable cause" – i.e., the standard which must be met for an indictment – to match the higher, "reasonable doubt" standard required for a conviction.[91] Therefore, it "strongly disagree[d] with the court's analysis in *Pool*" regarding the extent to which arrest and indictment diminish a person's reasonable expectation of privacy.[92]

Issues Courts are Likely to Consider in Future Cases

Courts will likely wrestle with the questions raised by the divergent *Pool* and *Marshall* decisions in future cases involving pre-conviction DNA collection. Several additional issues are likely to affect courts' analyses in such cases, and might also impact the existing judicial consensus regarding the constitutionality of DNA collection from persons who have been convicted of a crime. In particular, the emerging science regarding biological purposes for junk DNA and the FBI's long-term storage of DNA profiles are likely to play a role in future analyses.

New Research on Junk DNA

Despite the "rapid pace of technological development in the area of DNA analysis,"[93] much of DNA's scientific value remains a mystery. As mentioned, FBI analysts rely on junk DNA, thought not to reveal sensitive medical or biological information. Partly for that reason, proponents of expansive DNA collection argue that any privacy intrusion resulting from DNA storage or analysis is minimal at most. For example, when he introduced the amendment that authorizes collection and analysis of DNA from arrestees in the federal system, Senator Kyl emphasized that storage of DNA samples would not intrude upon individuals' privacy rights, stating that "the sample of DNA that is kept ... is what is called 'junk DNA' – it is impossible to determine anything medically sensitive from this DNA."[94] Likewise, courts have assumed that DNA analysis and storage involves only a minimal privacy intrusion.

However, language in some opinions suggest that this assumption might change if scientists discover new uses for junk DNA. For example, the U.S. Court of Appeals for the First Circuit has suggested that "discovery of new uses for 'junk DNA' would require a reevaluation of the [Fourth Amendment] reasonableness balance."[95]

Scientific research on junk DNA is still emerging, and some research suggests that junk DNA has more biological value than previously assumed. For example, in October 2008, University of Iowa researchers released study findings showing that junk DNA has the potential to "evolve into exons, which are the building blocks for protein-coding genes."[96] Other scientists have similarly argued that there might be "gems among the junk" in DNA.[97] Hence, a remaining question is whether use of junk DNA will continue to offer superficial identifying information or whether it will reveal more detailed medical or biological characteristics.

Storage of DNA Profiles after Punishment Ends

A final issue that might arise in future DNA cases is the constitutionality of storing convicts' DNA profiles after their sentences have ended. As mentioned, federal law requires the FBI to expunge DNA profiles for people who receive acquittals or whose convictions are overturned.[98] However, the expungement provisions do not address storage of DNA from people who have been convicted but have successfully completed their sentences. Rather, as the Ninth Circuit Court of Appeals noted in *United States v. Kriesel*, "once they have [a person's] DNA, police at any level of government with a general criminal investigative interest ... can tap into that DNA without any consent, suspicion, or warrant, long after his period of supervised release ends."[99] Defendants have generally not raised this issue, but it might become a more prevalent argument since laws have expanded collection authority to reach people convicted for relatively minor charges.

Some courts have signaled that storage after sentences are completed could alter the Fourth Amendment analysis. For example, in an opinion upholding collection of DNA from a person on supervised release, the U.S. Court of Appeals for the First Circuit warned that its opinion had an "important limitation." Namely, because the petitioner was "on supervised release and will remain so until 2009, [the court did] not resolve the question of whether it is also constitutional to retain the DNA profile in the database after he is no longer on supervised release."[100] Courts might be receptive to arguments regarding the long-term storage of DNA as an unconstitutional search, although some courts have upheld ongoing storage of fingerprints and other evidence.[101] The resolution of that question might depend in part on whether completion of a sentence is viewed as restoring a person's reasonable expectation of privacy.

CONCLUSION

Although nearly all courts that have addressed the issue have upheld the compulsory collection of DNA from persons who have been convicted, no judicial consensus has yet emerged regarding the constitutionality of such collection from persons who have been arrested or are facing charges prior to a criminal trial. The two U.S. district court cases addressing pre-conviction DNA collection illustrate that outcomes in future cases involving arrestees may depend on courts' resolution of at least two key issues, namely: (1) what, if any, distinction exists between the reasonable expectation of privacy of an arrestee and a convict; and (2) the degree of privacy intrusion perceived as a result of a DNA sample. The latter question may turn on courts' framing of the role of DNA collection – i.e., whether it is analogous to the long-upheld practice of fingerprinting or whether it represents a greater privacy intrusion.

Existing expungement provisions might also become a factor in future challenges to pre- conviction DNA collection. The government might argue that requirements that DNA samples be expunged once an arrestee is discharged or acquitted offset the degree of privacy intrusion caused by such samples. To date, some federal courts have made note of the expungement provisions,[102] but they generally have not addressed the effect of expungement requirements in Fourth Amendment analyses. Courts may be more likely to do so in future cases brought by arrestees.

Author Contact Information

Anna C. Henning
Legislative Attorney
ahenning@crs.loc.gov, 7-4067

End Notes

[1] For more on the progression of federal legislation authorizing use of DNA, see CRS Report RL32247, *DNA Testing for Law Enforcement: Legislative Issues for Congress*, by Nathan James.

[2] For example, offenses triggering DNA collection authority under the original DNA Analysis Backlog Elimination Act of 2000, P.L. 106-546 (2000), included: murder, voluntary manslaughter, and other offense relating to homicide; offenses relating to sexual abuse, sexual exploitation or other abuse of children, or transportation for illegal sexual activity; offenses relating to peonage and slavery; kidnapping; offenses involving robbery or burglary; certain offenses committed within Indian territory; and attempt or conspiracy to commit any of the above offenses.

[3] United States v. Kincade, 345 F.3d 1095, 1096 n.2 (9th Cir. 2003), *vac 'd and rehearing en banc granted*, 354 F.3d 1000 (9th Cir. 2003).

[4] Forensic scientists use "short tandem repeat" technology to analyze 13 DNA regions, or "loci." Although it is theoretically possible that two unrelated people could share identical DNA strands, "the odds that two individuals will have the same 13-loci DNA profile is about one in a billion." Department of Energy, *Human Genome Project Information: DNA Forensics*, at http://www.ornl.gov/sci/techresources/Human_Genome/elsi/forensics.shtml.

[5] *See* DNA-Sample Collection and Biological Evidence Preservation in the Federal Jurisdiction, 73 Fed. Reg. 74932, 74933 (Dec. 10, 2008) (to be codified at 28 C.F.R. pt. 28) ("DNA profiles, which embody information concerning 13 'core loci,' amount to 'genetic fingerprints' that can be used to identify an individual uniquely").

[6] Under federal statute and analogous state laws, officials collect DNA from "tissue, fluid, or other bodily sample." 42 U.S.C. §14135a(c)(1). To facilitate especially "reliable" DNA analysis, FBI guidelines direct federal law enforcement officials to rely on blood samples. See United States v. Kincade, 379 F.3d 813, 817 (9th Cir. 2004) (en banc).

[7] DNA-Sample Collection and Biological Evidence Preservation in the Federal Jurisdiction, 73 Fed. Reg. at 74933-34.

[8] The Combined DNA Index System includes a "hierarchy" of DNA-profile databases, including a National DNA Index System, which facilitates sharing of DNA profiles between participating law enforcement agencies throughout the country; a State DNA Index System, through which DNA profiles are shared throughout a state; and a Local DNA Index System, from which DNA profiles originate before being added to the higher-level indexing systems. Within these systems, profiles are categorized into offender profiles, arrestee profiles, and other categories. For a more detailed description of the system, see http://www.fbi.gov/hq/lab/html/codis1.htm.

[9] United States v. Amerson, 483 F.3d 73, 76 (2d Cir. 2007) (quoting H.R. Rep. No. 106-900 (2000)).

[10] *See Kincade*, 379 F.3d at 818; H.R. Rep. No. 106-900 at 27 (2000).

[11] As of February 2009, the federal government and all states except Idaho, Kentucky, Nebraska, New Hampshire, and Pennsylvania authorized DNA collection from people convicted of any felony. See National Conference of State Legislatures, *State Laws on DNA Data Banks: Qualifying Offenses, Others Who Must Provide Sample* (Feb. 2009), at http://www.ncsl.org/default.aspx?tabid=12737.

[12] 42 U.S.C. § 14135a.

[13] *Id.* at § 14135a(a)(4)(A).

[14] *See* National Conference of State Legislatures, *State Laws on DNA Data Banks: Qualifying Offenses, Others Who Must Provide Sample* (Feb. 2009), at http://www.ncsl.org/default.aspx?tabid=12737 (indicating that as of 2008, 15 states had authorized DNA collection from arrestees).

[15] P.L. 103-322, 108 Stat. 2065 (1994) (codified at 42 U.S.C. §§ 14131-14134).

[16] P.L. 104-132, 110 Stat. 1214 (1996).

[17] P.L. 105-251, 112 Stat. 1871 (1998).

[18] See *http://www.fbi.gov/hq/lab/codis/clickmap.htm.*

[19] 42 U.S.C. § 14135a(a)(1)(B).

[20] P.L. 106-546, § 3, 114 Stat. 2726, 2729-30 (2000).

[21] P.L. 107-56, § 503, 115 Stat. 272, 364 (2001).

[22] P.L. 108-405, § 203(b), 118 Stat. 2260, 2270 (2004) (codified at 42 U.S.C. § 14135a(a)(2)).

[23] *See* National Conference of State Legislatures, *State Laws on DNA Data Banks: Qualifying Offenses, Others Who Must Provide Sample* (Feb. 2009), at http://www.ncsl.org/default.aspx?tabid=12737.

[24] DNA Fingerprint Act of 2005, Tit. X, P.L. 109-162, 119 Stat. 2960. 42 U.S.C. § 14135a(a)(1).

[25] Adam Walsh Child Protection and Safety Act of 2006, sec. 155, P.L. 109-248, 120 Stat. 587 (2006) (codified at 42 U.S.C. § 14135a(a)(1)).

[26] DNA-Sample Collection and Biological Evidence Preservation in the Federal Jurisdiction, 73 Fed. Reg. at 74,932, 74,935.

[27] 28 C.F.R. § 28.12(b).

[28] *See, e.g.*, Kan. Stat. Ann. § 21-25 11(e)(2) (authorizing DNA collection from individuals arrested for any felony or certain other crimes); N.M. Stat. § 29-16-6(B) (authorizing collection of DNA samples from individuals arrested for specific violent felonies); Va.

Code Ann. § 19.2-310.2:1 (requiring collection of DNA samples from "arrested for the commission or attempted commission of a violent felony").

[29] 151 Cong. Rec. S13756 (daily ed. Dec. 16, 2005) (statement of Sen. Kyl).

[30] DNA-Sample Collection and Biological Evidence Preservation in the Federal Jurisdiction, 73 Fed. Reg. at 74,934.

[31] 42 U.S.C. § 14132(d).

[32] *Id.* However, no provision requires expungement of DNA upon a convict's completion of his or her sentence.

[33] U.S. Const. amend. IV.

[34] Courts have applied the Fourth Amendment to state and local government actions since 1961, when, in *Mapp v. Ohio*, the Supreme Court interpreted the Fourteenth Amendment as having incorporated the Fourth Amendment to the states. 367 U.S. 643, 655 (1961).

[35] *See* United States v. Place, 462 U.S. 696, 716 (1983) (Brennan, J., concurring in result); Michigan v. Summers, 452 U.S. 692, 696 (1981).

[36] Some justices and experts have noted the circularity of the combination of this definition and the general Fourth Amendment "reasonableness" inquiry. *See, e.g.*, Minnesota v. Carter, 525 U.S. 83, 97 (1998) (Scalia, J., concurring). However, such criticisms have not yet caused the Court to reconsider its test, except perhaps for the narrow category of interiors of homes, for which the Court has found a near-automatic reasonable expectation of privacy by virtue of privacy in the home having "roots deep in the common law." *See* Kyllo v. United States, 533 U.S. 27, 34 (2001).

[37] *Kyllo*, 533 U.S. at 33 (citing California v. Ciraolo, 476 U.S. 207, 211 (1986)).

[38] Katz v. United States, 389 U.S. 347, 351 (1967).

[39] See, e.g., Davis v. Mississippi, 394 U.S. 721, 727 (1969) ("Fingerprinting involves none of the probing into an individual's private life and thoughts that marks an interrogation or search."). Later, in *Hayes v. Florida*, the Supreme Court seemed to suggest that fingerprinting does constitute a search, 470 U.S. 811, 814 (1985) (referring to fingerprinting as less intrusive than *other* types of searches and seizures), a shift in keeping with the Court's broader trend toward classifying more activity as constituting a search and leaving the heart of the constitutional analysis for the Fourth Amendment "reasonableness" inquiry. Thus, it appears that although the Court views the drawing of blood as a greater intrusion than fingerprinting, both activities now qualify as searches.

[40] *See, e.g.*, Skinner v. Ry. Labor Executives' Ass'n, 489 U.S. 602, 616 (1989) ("We have long recognized that a 'compelled intrusio[n] into the body for blood to be analyzed for alcohol content' must be deemed a Fourth Amendment search" (quoting Schmerber v. California, 384 U.S. 757, 767-768 (1966)). This distinction contrasts with the Supreme Court's rejection of a blood-versus-fingerprints distinction in the context of the confrontation clause to the Sixth Amendment of the U.S. Constitution, wherein the Court has held neither fingerprinting nor the taking of blood are barred because they are both "real and physical" rather than "testimonial" evidence. *See* Pennsylvania v. Muniz, 496 U.S. 582, 591 (1990).

[41] 534 U.S. 112, 119-120 (2001).

[42] *Id.*

[43] *Id.* at 118.

[44] *See, e.g.*, Atwater v. City of Lago Vista, 532 U.S. 318, 354 (2001) (recognizing a warrant exception for arrest of an individual who commits a crime in an officer's presence, as long as the arrest is supported by probable cause).

[45] Illinois v. Gates, 462 U.S. 213, 232 (1983).

[46] *Id.* at 238.

[47] 392 U.S. 1, 7 (1968).

[48] *Id.* at 21-22, 27.

[49] Alabama v. White, 496 U.S. 325, 330 (1990) ("[r]easonable suspicion is a less demanding standard than probable cause").

[50] Samson v. California, 547 U.S. 843, 848 (2006).

[51] Griffin v. Wisconsin, 483 U.S. 868, 873 (1986) (citing New Jersey v. T.L.O., 469 U.S. 325, 351 (1985) (Blackmun, J., concurring)).

[52] *Id.* at 873-74.

[53] 534 U.S. 112, 114 (2001).

[54] *Id.*

[55] *Id.* at 115.

[56] *Id.* at 119-20. (noting that "just as other punishments for criminal convictions curtail an offender's freedoms, a court granting probation may impose reasonable conditions that deprive the offender of some freedoms enjoyed by law- abiding citizens" and concluding that "the probation condition thus significantly diminished Knight's reasonable expectation of privacy").

[57] *Id.* at 119, 12 1-22 (after discussing the interests on both sides of the general reasonableness test, holding "that the balance of these considerations requires no more than reasonable suspicion to conduct a search of petitioner's house").

[58] 547 U.S. 843 (2006).

[59] *Id.* at 848. In parts, the *Knights* opinion appeared to suggest that conditions explicitly imposed upon the probationer, rather than the probationer's status itself, created the diminished privacy expectation. However, in a footnote, the Knights court signaled its support for the rationale, later adopted in Samson, that post-conviction status itself diminishes a probationer's or a parolee's expectation of privacy. Specifically, the *Knights* Court cited the Wisconsin Supreme Court's holding in *Griffin* that "'probation diminishes a probationer's reasonable expectation of privacy – so that a probation officer may, consistent with the Fourth Amendment, search a probationer's home without a warrant, and with only 'reasonable grounds' (not probable cause) to believe that contraband is present." *Knights*, 534 U.S. at 118 n.3 (citing *Griffin*, 483 U.S. at 872.).

[60] *Samson*, 547 U.S. at 850-52.

[61] *Samson*, 547 U.S. at 850 (quoting *Knights*, 534 U.S. at 119).

[62] *See Samson*, 547 U.S. at 852 (quoting Morrissey v. Brewer, 408 U.S. 471, 477 (1972)).

[63] *See, e.g.*, *Wilson*, 517 F.3d at 426-27 ("a parolee ... has less diminished privacy rights than a prisoner").

[64] *See, e.g.*, United States v. Amerson, 483 F.3d 73, 77 (2d Cir. 2007) ("It is settled law that DNA indexing statutes, because they authorize both a physical intrusion to obtain a tissue sample and a chemical analysis to obtain private physiological information about a person, are subject to the strictures of the Fourth Amendment.").

[65] *See, e.g.*, United States v. Kincade, 345 F.3d 1095, 1100 n. 13 (9th Cir. 2003) ("Although the taking of blood may properly be characterized as a Fourth Amendment seizure, because it interferes with [the appellant's] 'possessory interest in his bodily fluids,' for present purposes we consider only the search, and note that the 'privacy expectations protected by this [the seizure] are adequately taken into account by our conclusion that such intrusions are searches") (quoting Skinner v. Ry. Labor Executives Ass'n, 489 U.S. 602, 617 n.4 (1989)).

[66] One exception is the panel decision of the U.S. Court of Appeals for the Ninth Circuit in *United States v. Kincade*, which was later overturned in an en banc decision. 345 F.3d 1095 (9th Cir. 2003), vac'd and rehearing en banc granted, 354 F.3d 1000 (9th Cir. 2003).

[67] The Supreme Court has addressed the separate issue of defendants' post-conviction access to DNA evidence. *See, e.g.*, District Attorney's Office for the Third Judicial District v. Osborne, 129 S. Ct. 2308 (2009).

[68] United States v. Weikert, 504 F.3d 1 (1st Cir. 2007); United States v. Amerson, 483 F.3d 73 (2d Cir. 2007); Wilson v. Collins, 517 F.3d 421 (6th Cir. 2006); United States v. Hook, 471 F.3d 766 (7th Cir. 2006); United States v. Kraklio, 451 F.3d 922 (8th Cir. 2006); United States v. Kriesel, 508 F.3d 941 (9th Cir. 2007); United States v. Banks, 490 F.3d 1178 (10th Cir. 2007); United States v. Castillo-Lagos, 147 Fed. App'x. 71 (11th Cir. 2005).

[69] Padgett v. Donald, 401 F.3d 1273 (1 1th Cir. 2005) (upholding the Georgia statute); Green v. Berge, 354 F.3d 675 (7th Cir. 2004) (upholding the Wisconsin statute); Shaffer v. Saffle, 148 F.3d 1180 (10th Cir. 1998) (upholding the Oklahoma statute); Schlicher v. Peters, 103 F.3d 940 (10th Cir. 1996) (upholding the Kansas statute); Boling v. Romer, 101 F.3d 1336 (10th Cir. 1996) (upholding the Colorado statute); Jones v. Murray, 962 F.2d 302 (4th Cir. 1992) (upholding the Virginia statute).

[70] *See* United States v. Kraklio, 451 F.3d 922, 924 (8th Cir. 2006) ("The only disagreement among the circuits is what analytical approach to use in upholding the [DNA collection] statutes.").

[71] *Contrast* United States v. Weikert, 504 F.3d 1, 7 (1st Cir. Aug. 9, 2007); United States v. Banks, 490 F.3d 1178, 1183 (10th Cir. 2007); United States v. Kraklio, 451 F.3d 922, 924 (8th Cir. 2006); United States v. Castillo-Lagos, 147 Fed. App'x 71 (1 1th Cir. 2005) *with* United States v. Amerson, 483 F.3d 73, 78 (2d Cir. 2007); United States v. Hook, 471 F.3d 766, 772-74 (7th Cir. 2006). The Sixth Circuit has upheld the federal DNA collection law under both tests. United States v. Conley, 453 F.3d 674, 677-8 1 (6th Cir. 2006).

[72] 517 F.3d 421, 426 (6th Cir. 2008).

[73] 504 F.3d 1, 3 (1st Cir. 2007) ("We interpret the Supreme Court's decision in *Samson v. California* to require that we join the majority of the circuits in applying a 'totality of the circumstances' approach to the issues in this case, rather than the 'special needs' analysis used by the minority of circuits" (citations omitted)). Similarly, some state courts have interpreted *Samson* as applicable in compulsory DNA collection cases. For example, despite continuing to apply the special needs test in DNA cases, the Supreme Court of New Jersey recognized that "the most recent United States Supreme Court decision in *Samson* strongly suggests that the balancing test, which is an easier test for the State to satisfy, should apply to a Fourth Amendment analysis." State v. O'Hagen, 189 N.J. 140, 158 (2007).

[74] 483 F.3d at 73, 79 (2d Cir. 2007).

[75] *Id.* ("while after *Samson* it can no longer be said that 'the Supreme Court has never applied a general balancing test to a suspicionless-search regime,' nothing in Samson suggests that a general balancing test should replace special needs as the primary mode of analysis of suspicionless searches outside the context of the highly diminished expectation of privacy presented in *Samson*") (quoting its previous opinion, Nicholas v. Goord, 430 F.3d 652, 666 (2d Cir. 2005)).

[76] *Wilson*, 517 F.3d at 426 (noting that cases involving petitioners on supervised release had declined to follow *Samson*).

[77] 547 U.S. at 847.

[78] *See, e.g.*, *Wilson*, 517 F.3d at 427 n. 4 ("Even if we were to apply the more stringent special-needs test, there is no reason to believe the ultimate result would be different.").

[79] *See, e.g.*, United States v. Kriesel, 508 F.3d 941, 948-49 (9th Cir. 2007) ("We emphasize that our ruling today does not cover DNA collection from arrestees or non-citizens detained in the custody of the United States, who are required to submit to DNA collection by the 2006 version of the DNA Act").

[80] This report focuses on federal court decisions, but several state courts have also reviewed the collection of DNA from arrestees. For example, in Anderson v. Virginia, 650 S.E.2d 702 (Vir. 2006), the Virginia Supreme Court upheld Virginia's statute authorizing DNA collection from arrestees. It analogized the collection of DNA samples to the routine taking of fingerprints, emphasizing that collecting such samples necessitated only a minimal privacy intrusion. *Id.* at 706. It rejected the defendant's assertion that the special needs test applied. Instead, it applied the general balancing test and concluded that the "same rationale" tipped the balance in the government's favor as applied to collection of DNA from convicted felons. *Id.* ("In the case of convicted felons who are in custody of the Commonwealth ... the minor intrusion caused by the taking of a [DNA] sample is outweighed by Virginia's interest ... in determining inmates' 'identification characteristics'" (quoting Jones v. Murray, 962 F.2d 302, 307 (Va. 1992)).

[81] 645 F. Supp.2d 903 (E.D.Cal. 2009).

[82] 2009 U.S. Dist. LEXIS 103575 (2009).

[83] In *Pool*, the defendant was granted pre trial release. For that reason, a provision of the Bail Reform Act, 18 U.S.C. § 3142(b), which requires DNA collection as a condition of pre-trial release, provided a supplementary basis of statutory authority.

[84] Both courts discussed but declined to apply the special needs test. They noted that a minority of federal courts of appeals have applied the special needs test in DNA collection cases and expressed doubt that the DNA collection statutes served a special need beyond law enforcement purposes. *See, e.g.*, *Mitchell*, 2009 U.S. Dist. LEXIS 103575 at *18 ("The legislative intent fails to suggest that the enactment of the DNA collection statutes was based upon any special need outside of law enforcement purposes").

[85] *Pool*, 645 F. Supp.2d at 911.

[86] *Mitchell*, 2009 U.S. Dist. LEXIS 103575 at *28.

[87] *Pool*, 645 F. Supp.2d at 911.

[88] *Mitchell*, 2009 U.S. Dist. LEXIS 103575 at *31.

[89] *Pool*, 645 F. Supp.2d at 909.

[90] *Pool*, 645 F. Supp.2d at 905 (limiting its holding to cases where collection occurs "after a judicial or grand jury determination of probable cause has been made for felony criminal charges against a defendant").

[91] *Mitchell*, 2009 U.S. Dist. LEXIS 103575 at *23.

[92] *Id.*

[93] United States v. Weikert, 504 F.3d 1, 3 (1st Cir. 2007).

[94] 151 Cong. Rec. S13757 (daily ed. Dec. 16, 2005) (statement of Sen. Kyl).

[95] United States v. Stewart, 532 F.3d 32, 36 (1st Cir. 2008).

[96] Lin L, Shen S, Tye A, Cai JJ, Jiang P, et al. *Diverse Splicing Patterns of Exonized Alu Elements in Human Tissues*. PLoS Genet 4(10): e1000225. doi:10. 1371/journal.pgen. 1000225 (2008), at http://www.plos.org/press/plge-04-10-17- xing.pdf.

[97] W. Wayt Gibbs. *The Unseen Genome: Gems Among the Junk*. Sci. Am. 29 (Nov. 2003).

[98] 42 U.S.C. § 14132(d).

[99] 508 F.3d 941, 952 (9th Cir. 2007).

[100] *Weikert*, 504 F.3d at 2.

[101] *See, e.g.*, Stevenson v. United States, 380 F.2d 590 (D.C. Cir.), *cert. denied*, 389 U.S. 962 (1967) (holding that a defendant had no constitutional right to the expungement of his mugshots and fingerprints after his conviction was set aside).

[102] *See, e.g.*, United States v. Sczubelek, 402 F.3d 175, 187 (3d. Cir. 2005), *cert. denied*, 548 U.S. 919 (2006).

CHAPTER SOURCES

Chapter 1 is an edited, excerpted and augmented edition of a Congressional Research Service publication, CRS Report for Congress Order Code RL31826 Updated June 29, 2009.

Chapter 2 is an edited, excerpted and augmented edition of a Congressional Research Service publication, CRS Report for Congress Order Code RL34404 Updated Novemner 16, 2009.

Chapter 3 is an edited, excerpted and augmented edition of a Congressional Research Service publication, CRS Report for Congress Order Code RL34424 Updated February 2, 2010.

Chapter 4 is an edited, excerpted and augmented edition of a Congressional Research Service publication, CRS Report for Congress Order Code R40189 Updated February 2, 2009.

Chapter 5 is an edited, excerpted and augmented edition of a Congressional Research Service publication, CRS Report for Congress Order Code R40676 Updated June 29, 2009.

Chapter 6 is an edited, excerpted and augmented edition of a Congressional Research Service publication, CRS Report for Congress Order Code RL34624 Updated August 19, 2008.

Chapter 7 is an edited, excerpted and augmented edition of a Congressional Research Service publication, CRS Report for Congress Order Code R40077 Updated February 16,2010.

INDEX

H

I

J

K

L

M

N

O

P

Q

U

V

W

X